Say YES!

Gary Heyes

Acknowledgments

Thank you for every pastor and church for allowing me to share these thoughts and for responding to the Holy Spirit as He touched your hearts.

Thank you to my wife Sheila who always encourages me to live my dreams.

Thank you to Mary Ann Meyer, Gillian Dias, Nicky Robyn, Charlene Groen and Sheila Heyes for editing & helpful insights.

Thank you Melissa Heyes for the cover.

Table of Contents

"What Are You Saying YES to?"

On New Years Eve of 2014, my pastor asked this question. He was preaching about vision. That night, the Holy Spirit began to work the question deep into my heart: *What are you saying yes to?* This has become a defining question for me.

As I meditated on this, the Holy Spirit began to point out things that I was saying YES to that were producing some great things in my heart and life. However, He also pointed out that I was also saying YES to things and people that were hindering me from obtaining my destiny. I have come to understand that we can give permission to many things in our lives that can either help or hinder us from moving toward our destiny.

God wants to empower us to say YES, and what we say YES to will define our future. Saying YES to the things that God wants for our lives can even impact future generations to come.

So my friend, "What are you saying yes to?" Throughout this book, we will look at many areas in which we need to say YES. Each of the following areas represent significant principles we need to address in our lives.

- *Before you say YES say NO!*
- *Say YES to Your Identity in Christ*
- *Say YES to the Promises of God*
- *Say YES to a Prosperous Soul*
- *Say YES to Being Shaken*
- *Say YES to the Good Fight*
- *Say YES to Your Place*
- *Say YES to the House of God*
- *Say YES to Reaching One Person at a Time*

I want to encourage you to allow the Holy Spirit entrance in your life. Allow Him to put a resounding YES in your spirit! Evaluate the areas of your life that you are saying YES to and make sure that this is what God would desire for you.

Before You Say YES—Say NO!

"Brethren, I do not count myself to have apprehended; but one thing I do, forgetting those things which are behind and reaching forward to those things which are ahead." (Philippians 3:13, NKJV)

In early 2015, I was asked to do a funeral for a family that I didn't know. I always like to meet with the family to assess the situation and find out how they would like me to frame the service for their deceased loved one. Immediately, the boyfriend made it clear that he wasn't religious and didn't want any "God stuff".

Within the last year, the girlfriend had lost a number of friends and family members. Her brother, who was the deceased, was her last living relative and had been killed tragically. This woman was really struggling and began to share how she couldn't get past the previous loss of her father and mother.

I always try to be sensitive to the Holy Spirit in these situations, as it is a great opportunity to minister healing and speak life into tender, hurting hearts. The thought came to me that "for every ending there is a new beginning." I began to speak to this woman about how I believed that this was a new opportunity for her to start fresh and to move forward in her life—that although this was a difficult time, it could be the start of something new. I told her that, perhaps, God wanted her to use this moment to leave her pain and loss behind and move into her future holding only good memories.

Her boyfriend looked at me and began to chime in, "That's right. Keep going!"

I shared the principle of say YES to the right things and allowing peace to take over. The next day, right before the funeral was to start, the boyfriend called me over and said,

"What you said to my girlfriend really helped her. We want to get married but we have to leave some issues behind. Could you meet with us and help us?"

I said, "YES!" We met a number of times. I ended up officiating their wedding ceremony them and watched them enter into their new life together, enjoying happiness and greater peace.

It might seem like a contradiction, but although this book is about saying YES to many things, I have found that in order to say YES to God's best, we have to also say NO to many things. There are certain things, situations and people that will hinder us from reaching our destiny and becoming our best.

God wants us to live from a place of our best!

Say NO to Your Past

We need to say NO to **our past ruling over us**.

The Apostle Paul is a great example of this. He was a zealot. He put Christians in jail and even killed some of them. After his encounter with Jesus, he had to say NO to his past and begin the journey toward his future. He could have easily allowed his past to hinder or cripple him from the joys of serving God but he decided to leave it behind and look forward.

"No, dear brothers and sisters, I have not achieved it, but I focus on this one thing: Forgetting the past and looking forward to what lies ahead." (Philippians 3:13, NLT)

When I was a young man, I fell away from the Lord and did some things I'm not proud of. Every once in a while, the enemy will try to bring these to my mind in order to bring condemnation, shame and guilt. His intent is to limit me and hold me back from my future. I must determine to not allow this.

The enemy—and even well-meaning people—will want to remind you of your past. They bring up things that were dealt with many years ago and, sometimes quite subtly, you are reminded of your weaknesses and hindered from moving forward. Many of us relive our past mistakes, failures or even successes but miss the future because of a lack of focus. We need to say NO to letting the grip of our past control our lives. I would encourage you not to listen to the voices that would keep you down. Say NO to your past.

Say NO to Insecurity

We need to say NO to **insecurity.** We all have insecurity in our lives. The question is, will we allow it to control us and hinder us from saying YES to God's purposes?

I have had to deal with my fair share of insecurity in my life. As a young man, I was ridiculed publicly by well-meaning teachers who told me that I wasn't going to amount to anything they labeled me a certain type of person without knowing anything about the struggles I was facing.

As a result, however, I learned some things about the nature of insecurity.

Insecurity will try to silence your voice and limit your spirit. When you are silent, you don't speak up. You retreat and feel small around others. Before long, your spirit begins to shrink and vital resources are depleted.

Insecurity needs to be faced head on. Sometimes you have to stand up to the bully. So speak up! Declare God's promises over your life, and surround yourself with people who inspire, who celebrate you, who speak the truth in love to you because they believe in you.

Insecurity will cause you to live in the comparison game. When you compare yourself to others, it's often because you feel small and you want to elevate your accomplishments so you feel bigger.

But this actually has the opposite effect. Sometimes we engineer ourselves to stay small instead of taking steps towards growth and vitality.

Insecurity is a trap that will ultimately limit you from being grateful for others and celebrating diversity in people. When you live in insecurity you can't rejoice when someone is promoted or elevated because you want what they have.

Insecurity can push you to become loud and aggressive. When we are loud and aggressive, we attack. We want to become the center of conversations and we look to always compliment ourselves. We look to shut others down or speak ill of them to elevate ourselves. Insecure people can become defensive and judgmental, taking things personally. Many times they can begin to threaten and intimidate people to get their point across.

Don't give your time or energy to these types of people. Strive to become someone who always encourages others, building them up in their faith. We are prophetic people who should function with the goal to edify, encourage and comfort one another.

"But one who prophesies strengthens others, encourages them, and comforts them." (1 Corinthians 14:3, NLT)

A few years ago, I attended a conference and the speaker, Dennis Lacheney, spoke on insecurity. He gave 21 traits of insecurity in leaders, and he was gracious enough to allow me to use this material.

Insecure leaders:

1. Defend when they should explore.
2. Take things personally.
3. Blame higher ups for tough decisions.
4. Don't trust others because they don't trust themselves.
5. Can't say no.
6. Threaten, intimidate, and coerce.
7. Shut down input from others because feedback is frightening.
8. Micromanage.
9. Won't delegate.
10. Create teams of yes-men.
11. Illustrate their competence and successes too frequently.
12. Hoard knowledge.
13. Backstab.
14. Delay decisions and then flip flop after.
15. Seem snobbish.
16. Crave positional authority and respect.

17. Nitpick and belittle.
18. Share blame and take credit.
19. Name drop.
20. Think others are out to get them.[1]

Each of these areas could be a point of discussion, but I would like to encourage you to evaluate your life and see if any apply. If they do, ask the Holy Spirit to release them from you heart and say NO to the grip of insecurity over your life.

Say NO to Fear and Worry

"God has not given us a spirit of fear but of love, power and a sound mind." (2 Timothy 1:7, NKJV)

"Be anxious for nothing, but in everything by prayer and supplication, with thanksgiving, let your requests be made known to God." (Philippians 4:6, NKJV)

We need to say NO to **fear and worry.** God calls us to cast our care upon Him, to not worry or be anxious for anything.

What is anxiety?

- Anxiety is built on what might happen. It affects every area of your life, and thrives on the "what ifs".

- Anxiety and fear reveal a lack of confidence and hope in a good and faithful God.

- Anxiety can lead to your perspective being blown out of proportion. Small things seem huge and molehills turn into unbeatable mountains.

If negativity rather than good words and thoughts are in your heart, it will lead to anxiety. Anxiety has the capacity to decline into depression: "Anxiety in the heart of man causes depression, but a good word makes it glad" (Proverbs 12:25, NKJV).

Giving into defeated thoughts—allowing them to linger in your mind and occupy your soul—will eventually plunge you into a bottomless pit of depression and fear.

Fear can cripple you, it will mock you and intimidate you by speaking limitations over your life.

Have you ever been in a situation or circumstance that you could not get free from, such as debt, a toxic relationship, a bad job or a nagging health issue? The enemy wants to cause that issue to take control of your mind and heart.

He wants to cause that issue to consume your thinking and ravage your emotions. We need to allow the peace of God to take hold of our hearts and minds and say NO to that issue controlling us any further.

Perhaps the biggest fear you can face is the fear of the unknown. I have had moments when I was not sure when the next pay cheque was coming or when I faced the fear of being alone.

There are many times in life when we face the unknown. Each of these are opportunities for us to trust in a good God who is in control of every detail of our lives.

Remember, God's Word and Spirit are greater than anything we will ever face. His Word and Spirit can bring liberation to us.

Say NO to Laziness and Undisciplined Living

Over the years, I gained a few extra pounds and became lazy in my habits of exercise and eating. I decided to say NO to undisciplined living. I began to take small steps to get healthy and lose that nagging weight. Slowly, I began to change what I was eating and began to walk one mile then two.

I began to get healthier and more disciplined and started to lose weight. Now I walk about four to five miles a day and have lost 30 pounds.

What about you? How important is your health? God wants you along for the long haul! Decide today to say NO to unhealthy eating and say yes to living longer. What steps can you take today to say **NO to laziness and undisciplined living?**

Say NO to Negative Voices

Many different people can invade our space. Some voices speak affirmation and love while others will regularly point out our weaknesses and speak negativity into our lives. I'm all for someone seeing something in your life that can hurt you and pointing that out, but that should not be the only thing they are doing. They should also be encouraging you and speaking about your destiny.

There will always be "haters" or people who are jealous of our success. We need to walk away from these people. **Say NO to letting others shaping your perception, identity and destiny in a negative way.** It's important to be around people who celebrate you and encourage you toward your destiny.

"Life is too short, your destiny too great, your assignment too important to spend it with people who always pull you down." (Joel Osteen)[2]

One day, while I was in prayer, the Lord spoke clearly to my heart that I had been allowing a **spirit of negativity** in my life and that He wanted to break it from me. I was allowing the enemy's lies to infiltrate my mind, causing me to live at times with discouragement and disappointment. The recording in my mind was negative, the arguments were intense and I was living well below the level of grace that God had supplied. I was critical and living internally in defeat.

I began to say NO to negativity and God began to heal and deliver me. I began to reprogram my mind with what God thought about me and what His purpose was for my life.

I determined to no longer listen to the voice of negativity.

"And do not be conformed to this world, but be transformed by the renewing of your mind, that you may prove what is that good and acceptable and perfect will of God." (Romans 12:2, NKJV)

I began to stop my negative thoughts before they became higher thoughts and then arguments. I began to evict the enemy from my life and allow the Holy Spirit to develop new strongholds by placing God's promises and Word in my life. A new freedom took place and I began to have vision and develop a new hope for the future. Say NO to negativity in your life and watch what God will do.

"For though we walk in the flesh, we do not war according to the flesh. For the weapons of our warfare are not carnal but mighty in God for pulling down strongholds, casting down arguments and every high thing that exalts itself against the knowledge of God, bringing every thought into captivity to the obedience of Christ." (2 Corinthians 10:3-5, NKJV)

We are about to look at key areas in which you need to say YES. Before we do, please evaluate where you need to say NO. Allow the Holy Spirit to point out those areas in which the enemy has spoken lies that are holding you back from your destiny. Say NO in your spirit and begin to say YES to your future! Say YES to God doing new things in your life.

Say Yes to your Identity in Christ

"Therefore, if anyone is in Christ, he is a new creation the old has passed away; behold, the new has come." (2 Corinthians 5:17, NKJV)

Avoid the unhealthy extremes of being either too driven by your own ego or too self-deprecating. Instead, pray for God to help you see yourself as He sees you. When you have the humility to recognize that you must depend on God to do anything that matters, and when you have the confidence to recognize that God made you in His image for great purposes and deeply loves you, then you'll be free to live in ways fuelled by a burning passion to follow where God leads you." (E. Glenn Wagner)[1]

One of the most important lessons I've learned is to say YES to my identity in Christ. Much of the dysfunction happening in the world today is due in part to a loss of identity. We don't really know who we are anymore. There has been a shift in our thinking.

We have tried to develop our own understanding of who we are and we have made a mess of it.

Identity is defined as "the collective aspect of the set of characteristics by which a thing is definitively recognizable or known". A further definition of identity is "the quality or condition of being the same as something else". www.dictionary.com

In Genesis 3, we see that God created man and woman in His image and purposed them for great things. He gave them tasks to do and established a regular pattern of divine interaction. God gave one command: Don't eat of the tree of knowledge of good and evil. When Adam and Eve sinned by disobeying this command, they immediately fell into darkness.

There are some things that God never intended for us to know. He wanted us to be marked by certain characteristics that only He could provide. He wants to be our source of light and knowledge. What He wanted to provide would put a deep security and identification in our soul, a wholeness and safety!

Adam and Eve's lives were to be marked by the presence of a good God who was willing to provide everything they needed. Their lives and identity were to be defined by HIS PRESENCE, which would be a garment covering them.

Psalm 104:2 says, "God covers Himself with light as with a garment." Matthew 17:2 implies that light can be a garment for the righteous. I would like to suggest that Adam and Eve were previously clothed in God's glorious presence and light and the immediate loss of this covering of light and presence left them feeling insecure, exposed and naked. They saw their nakedness and were suddenly aware of their need for covering. They had lost their identity. Their light went out and sin, darkness and anxiety entered the human situation.

Each of us tries to invent ways to cover our shame and nakedness and hide our real self, which has been marred by sin. *HIS presence is more than enough for what we need and face!*

Coming back to Jesus Christ actually renews our identity in Him and brings us back to a place where we are no longer marked by sin, insecurity, shame, vulnerability and anxiety— a place where we experience His covering. We begin to find out who we really are and what God has determined for us.

Our previous identity consisted of insecurity, fear and shame, but God wants to clothe us with a new garment. He wants to create an inner change that will eventually make its way to our outer life. He creates a divine exchange and we begin to see ourselves differently.

Your personal identity—how you see yourself—is often shaped by your early experiences in life. Maybe your parents said things to you as a child that made you doubt your worth. Maybe you were rejected or abused and that left a huge hole in your view of humanity and yourself.

Every single person longs for significance. We were created for significance but that one decision in the garden many years ago thrust us into an identity confusion. Take hope! God has the answers to who we are and He wants to restore His image back to our lives.

Our "identity issue" is an important part of living the abundant life. Jesus was able to face the incredible demands of His mission because He knew exactly who He was and who His Father was. He knew that He mattered to God, and that gave Him confidence to move purposefully in faith.

Roman 12:2 states, "....to be transformed by the renewing of your mind, that you may prove what is that good and acceptable and perfect will of God" (NKJV).

Paul encourages us to allow our minds to be renewed, which literally means to be renovated and changed from within. This renovation and renewal will create transformation, a complete change in who we are.

It is important to make sure that the quest for change is directed and guided by the Word of God. If you remember back in the garden, Adam and Eve went after the wrong tree. Instead of choosing life, they sought a knowledge separate from God. Unfortunately, this led to darkness, shame, confusion and an identity crisis.

Scripture continually encourages us to focus our attention on the person and knowledge of Jesus Christ. When we realize that our identity is found in knowing Him and understanding who He is and what He has done for us, our lives will be transformed. A new peace, security and freedom will begin to take hold of us and we will begin to find significance and purpose.

Are you willing to forsake everything to know Him?

I once thought these things were valuable, but now I consider them worthless because of what Christ has done. Yes, everything else is worthless when compared with the infinite value of knowing Christ Jesus my Lord. For his sake I have discarded everything else, counting it all as garbage, so that I could gain Christ. (Philippians 3:7-8, NLT)

Paul, prior to coming to know Christ, found his significance in his status and achievements much like we do today. The size of our house, how much money is in our bank account, what kind of car we drive, who we know and what we do are all areas from which we try to gain significance and security.

If we really want to find our true self and who we were created to be, we must be willing to give up our attachment to our possessions, old thinking and old ways of behaving and believing. We need to allow the Holy Spirit to focus our attention on Him! We need to grow in our knowledge of who Jesus is and what He has done for us.

When we focus our attention on Jesus, we can walk into our true identity and receive security and peace, experiencing His great love. This knowledge allows us to experience the acceptance and longing that we all desire. The effects are lasting and fruitful, impacting not only our own lives, but the lives of our family members and those around us.

Who is Jesus to you? In Matthew 16:13-20, there is a discourse between Jesus and His disciples:

When Jesus came into the region of Caesarea Philippi, He asked His disciples, saying, "Who do men say that I, the Son of Man, am?"

So they said, "Some say John the Baptist, some Elijah, and others Jeremiah or one of the prophets."

He said to them, "But who do you say that I am?"

Simon Peter answered and said, "You are the Christ, the Son of the living God."

Jesus answered and said to him, "Blessed are you, Simon Bar-Jonah, for flesh and blood has not revealed this to you, but My Father who is in heaven. And I also say to you that you are Peter, and on this rock I will build My church, and the gates of Hades shall not prevail against it. And I will give you the keys of the kingdom of heaven, and whatever you bind on earth will be bound in heaven, and whatever you loose on earth will be loosed in heaven."

Jesus asked two questions: "Who do MEN say that I am?" and "Who do YOU say that I am?"

What is your experience or view of Jesus? Who Jesus is becomes an important question to answer. If you are not sure who Jesus is, you will never really be certain of who you are or can be. Your identity and security are rooted in your knowledge of His identity. What Jesus looks like to you determines how you will live out your life.

Notice that Jesus didn't ask His disciples, "What do people think about the miracles? How do they like my teaching or preaching? Do they like my clothing or my hair?" His questions were quite different.

Jesus began by asking, "Who do men say that I am?" His disciples responded by saying, "Some say John the Baptist, Elijah, Jeremiah or one of the prophets."

John was a reformer. He was a change agent who called people to repent of their sins. Elijah was a radical prophet who confronted the corruption and evil of his day. He also did miracles and was very influential. Jeremiah was a weeping prophet who was regularly broken over the sins of God's people. He was compassionate and wanted the best for the children of Israel.

Once Jesus found out what the crowd had to say, He wanted those closest to Him to weigh in and declare who *they* thought He was. Peter, the boldest of them all, responded without hesitation, "You are the Christ, the Son of the Living God!"

Immediately Jesus responded, "Blessed are you, Simon Bar-Jonah, for flesh and blood has not revealed this to you, but My Father who is in heaven."

This is a pretty amazing story. Let's be clear. Jesus knew who He was. He wasn't trying to figure that out. He wanted to make sure that the men who He was spending time with on a daily basis were getting to know Him intimately.

Jesus' response to Peter is very important for us if we are going to come to an understanding of our identity and knowledge of Jesus Christ. First of all, Jesus says that knowing who He is can only come from a revelation from the Father. Once we receive that revelation, even greater revelation will come. We can't rest in our own thinking and platitudes. We must trust the Father.

When we understand who Jesus is, we gain a new sense of purpose and direction. Jesus said, "I will build my church and I will give you keys."

When we come to a revelation of who Jesus is and what He means to each of us personally, we can then understand His plan and how we fit into that purpose. He begins to give us authority. We receive keys to unlock the doors and chains that are holding people bound in sin. We are given the ability in Christ to bind the works of the enemy and, with our very words and declarations, defeat him.

Make it a quest to know who Jesus is. He loves you and wants to show you a great future. He wants to give you a powerful identity and purpose.

Say YES to the Promises of God

"For all the promises of God in Him are YES and in Him Amen, to the glory of God through us." (2 Corinthians 1:20, NKJV)

"The permanence of God's character guarantees the fulfillment of his promises." (A.W. Pink)[1]

"Deeds such as God has wrung are not to be admired for an hour and then forgotten, they are meant to be perpetual signs and instructive tokens to all coming generations, and especially are designed to confirm the faith of His people in the Divine love and to make them know that the Lord is gracious and full of compassion." (Charles Spurgeon)[2]

There are times, as people of faith, when God comes to invade our lives—prophetic moments in time where the Lord breaks in and challenges us, changes us, stretches us and speaks to us, altering the course of our lives forever.

The Lord in His wisdom designs these times to prove what is in our heart and spirit. How will we respond? What will be the condition of our attitude? How will we pass on what we have learned to others? God wants each and every one of us to extend our faith and, with a resounding cry, say YES to His promises for our lives.

The Scripture is replete with promises that God has given to us. However, a promise in the Word of God is not a promise unless God makes it real to you. Your faith is energized and strengthened in the process. A promise that becomes a revelation from the Father is the promise that defeats the enemy. Flesh and blood can't reveal it to you but only God.

A promise defined is:

- A declaration that something will or will not be done, given.
- An express assurance on which expectation is to be based.
- An expectation of good things to come. (www.dictionary.com)[3]

A promise can come to you when God speaks into your heart! It can be a word of Scripture, a dream, an impression or a thought.

"A Promise from God - it's when God goes into your future and brings back the word necessary to get you there." (Bill Johnson)[4]

"For I know the thoughts that I think toward you, says the Lord." (Jeremiah 29:11, NKJV)

"My thoughts are nothing like your thoughts, says the Lord. And my ways are far beyond anything you could imagine. For just as the heavens are higher than the earth, so my ways are higher than your ways and my thoughts higher than your thoughts. The rain and snow come down from the heavens and stay on the ground to water the earth. They

cause the grain to grow, producing seed for the farm and bread for the hungry. It is the same with my word. I send it out, and it always produces fruit. It will accomplish all I want it to, and it will prosper everywhere I send it." (Isaiah 55:8-11, NLT)

"How precious are your thoughts about me, O God. They cannot be numbered! I can't even count them; they outnumber the grains of sand! And when I wake up, you are still with me!" (Psalm 139:17-18, NLT)

God has many thoughts that He thinks towards us great thoughts and possibilities for our future. He wants His Word to come alive in our hearts! When He sends out His Word, it always produces fruit. It always accomplishes what He intended it to do and prosperity goes wherever He sends it.

Settle in your heart that God wants to do something BIG with your life! Saying YES to His promises will change how you view God.

Who is God to you? What's your perception or view of God? Who God is becomes an important question to answer.

"Is He for you or against you? Is God angry or mad at you? Is He aloof and distant? Unreachable? Are you spending your whole Christian life trying to please someone who can't be quite appeased? Is your life built on a structure of: "if I can only do this God will take notice?" Is He trustworthy? Does He keep His Word? Do you believe God is a good God? That God is for you? That He thinks great things about you and He wants you to succeed? Do you believe that His plan is always good for you? That He is in control? He is madly in love with you! He's consistently pursuing you? What God looks like to you determines how you live out your Christian life. How you relate to Him, how you relate to others, how you relate to the world around you all come out of your belief in who God is." (Brian Houston)[5]

What happens when things don't quite work out the way we want? Is God a liar? Is He unfaithful? The Scripture says that God does not lie. He is a faithful God who keeps His Word to His people.

"God is not a man, so he does not lie. He is not human, so he does not change his mind. Has he ever spoken and failed to act? Has he ever promised and not carried it through?" (Numbers 23:19, NLT)

"When God made his promise to Abraham, since there was no one greater for him to swear by, he swore by himself." (Hebrews 6:13, NIV)

"He has remembered his promise to love and be faithful to Israel. The ends of the earth have seen the victory of our God." (Psalm 98:3, NLT)

"He made heaven and earth, the sea, and everything in them. He keeps every promise forever." (Psalm 146:6, NLT)

The battle is for your mind and heart. Don't allow the voice of the enemy to say, "Has God said? Did God really say you would be...? Is God really your healer? Did God really say He would supply all your needs?"

Here are just a few of God's covenantal promises that He assures we will receive if we believe in Him:

> Promise of rest – Hebrews 4
> Promise of the Holy Spirit – Acts 2:38-39
> Promise of His coming - 2 Peter 3
> Promise that He will not leave or forsake us – Hebrews 13:5
> Promise to supply all our needs – Philippians 4:19
> Promise of a future and a hope – Jeremiah 29:11
> Promise of deliverance – Joel 2:28-32

Saying Yes to God's Promises requires bold faith

"So the promise is received by faith. It is given as a free gift. And we are all certain to receive it, whether or not we live according to the law of Moses, if we have faith like Abraham's. For Abraham is the father of all who believe. That is what the Scriptures mean when God told him, "I have made you the father of many nations." This happened because Abraham believed in the God who brings the dead back to life and who creates new things out of nothing.

"Even when there was no reason for hope, Abraham kept hoping—believing that he would become the father of many nations. For God had said to him, "That's how many descendants you will have!" And Abraham's faith did not weaken, even though, at about 100 years of age, he figured his body was as good as dead—and so was Sarah's womb. Abraham never wavered in believing God's promise. In fact, his faith grew stronger, and in this he brought glory to God. He was fully convinced that God is able to do whatever he promises.

And because of Abraham's faith, God counted him as righteous. And when God counted him as righteous, it wasn't just for Abraham's benefit. It was recorded for our benefit too, assuring us that God will also count us as righteous if we believe in him, the one who raised Jesus our Lord from the dead. He was handed over to die because of our sins, and he was raised to life to make us right with God." (Romans 4:16-25, NLT)

God creates new things out of nothing. Faith is saying YES to God and coming into agreement even when we don't yet see the promise fulfilled. Faith is what is needed to bring the promise into reality. It is hoping even when your circumstances give you no reason to hope. Abraham was fully convinced that God is able to do whatever He promised.

I have watched God fulfill His promises as I have stepped out in faith and believed Him for increase. It has required me to keep hoping even when everything around me has indicated the opposite. It is and always will be about developing new levels of trust in a faithful and great God.

Saying Yes to God's Promises requires waiting for God's timing

Great faith is often accompanied by great patience. I've found that when you receive a promise from God, the exact opposite than what was promised sometimes happens. At times, things can seem to take a turn for the worst. In those moments, we need to trust God and believe that His timing is always perfect.

And we desire that each one of you show the same diligence to the full assurance of hope until the end, that you do not become sluggish, but imitate those who through faith and patience inherit the promises.

For when God made a promise to Abraham, because He could swear by no one greater, He swore by Himself, saying "Surely blessing I will bless you, and multiplying I will multiply you." And so, after he had patiently endured, he obtained the promise. (Hebrews 6:11-15, NKJV)

There are always specific times and seasons in life that God has appointed, times for His promises to be fulfilled. Often, we are not ready to receive what God desires for us. He has to get us ready to contain what He wants for us.

"It's dangerous to want the progress without the process." *(Peter Toggs)[6]*

There is always a delay before the promise comes. During that time, God is stripping things out of our lives and adding things into our lives, making it possible to handle the reward of the promise.

Joseph endured much before the promise of God came to his life.

- Did God love Joseph any less when he was sold and mistreated by his family?
- Did God love him any less when He was misunderstood and faced unfair accusations?
- Did God love him any less when his was imprisoned in a dark and dreary dungeon?
- Did God love him any less when he was forgotten and hidden?
- Did God love him more when he was elevated and promoted?
- Did God love him more because He was able to save his family and the known world from famine?

Many times in the midst of the battle, the enemy can push into our minds certain lies. For example, that blessing indicates God's love and trouble indicates God's anger or disappointment. These lies can hinder us from learning valuable lessons that we can only gain through the process. God always loves us. His love is unconditional!

Our task is not to waver in unbelief or distrust; we must reject a wavering mentality that can grip our lives.

"No unbelief or distrust made him waver concerning the promise of God, but he grew strong and was empowered by faith as he gave praise and glory to God." (Romans 4:20, MSG)

"Let us hold fast the confession of our hope without wavering, for He who promised is faithful." (Hebrews 10:23, NKJV)

Waver, in the Greek, means "to make use of our own judgment and reasoning in discerning things".

To waver at the promise is to take into consideration the promise and all the difficulties that lie in the way of its accomplishment and to therefore dispute it.

You don't fully cast it off nor do you fully embrace it. You waver back and forth. *One minute you're in, the next you're not.*

In Galatians 6:9, we are encouraged to "not grow weary while doing good, for in due season we shall reap if we do not lose heart."

Saying Yes to God's Promises requires saying Yes to God's work in your life

"By his divine power, God has given us everything we need for living a godly life. We have received all of this by coming to know him, the one who called us to himself by means of his marvellous glory and excellence. And because of his glory and excellence, he has given us great and precious promises. These are the promises that enable you to share his divine nature and escape the world's corruption caused by human desires." (2 Peter 1:3-4, NKJV)

God wants to work in us His nature and presence so we can escape the corruption in the world that is caused by human desires.

"There is a promise over our lives that God wants to bring to pass, but he often has to take us through a repositioning phase first. It's confusing and heart wrenching because you know you're following him and his will for your life, but your expectations have been dashed on the rocks of hard times." (Sheryl Brady)[7]

Joseph allowed the word of the Lord to prove that he was worthy to receive what God had promised: He sent a man before them—Joseph—who was sold as a slave. They hurt his feet with fetters, he was laid in irons. Until the time that his word came to pass, the word of the Lord tested him. The king sent and released him, the ruler of the people let him go free. He made him lord of his house, and ruler of all his possessions, to bind his princes at his pleasure. (Psalm 105:17-22, NKJV)

After a time of testing, Joseph's word came to pass. Regardless of your circumstances, GOD's plans and promises haven't changed. In one day, Joseph was brought before the king and delivered.

We need to develop *a fighting YES spirit*. We have to be a people who will fight to see the promise of God come to pass in our lives.

In 2 Corinthians 7:1, we are instructed, "Therefore, having these promises, beloved, let us cleanse ourselves from all filthiness of the flesh and spirit, perfecting holiness in the fear of God." We have to be willing to fight against unbelief, doubt, discouragement, fear of failure and the "what ifs" of life. We must put aside our own reasoning and judgment and have faith, trust and rest in God. 2 Peter 1:5 says, "In view of all this, make every effort to respond to God's promises."

God's promises will bring about a change in who we are. Each of us will be stretched and developed into more that we can imagine. God will fashion you into the person He needs you to be. His promises have the power to take us where we are unable to go ourselves and to make us into who He desires us to be!

God does for us what we are incapable of doing ourselves. When we embrace God's promises for our lives, they change us, transform us, equip and strengthen us for the journey ahead.

In Joshua chapter one, Joshua was encouraged to be "strong, and courageous". He had to stand upon the promises of the Word of God. He was about to battle thirty-one kings, taking cities and possessing the Promised Land.

If we are to accomplish what we believe God has called and instructed us to do, we must stand on the promises of God.

BELIEVE GOD! BE STRONG AND COURAGEOUS!

If God has given you a promise and it is yet to come to pass, rest assured that God will be faithful to perform HIS good word to you. Philippians 1:6 says, "He will be faithful to complete that which He started."

The Place of Promise represents:

- A place of freedom
- A place of deliverance
- A place where things are flowing in and out of our lives
- A place where resources are readily available
- A place where enemies are destroyed both supernaturally and strategically
- A place where our faith is restored and increased
- A place of divine encounter.

The enemy does not want us to move into the place of promise! It signals his defeat in our lives. Will you say YES to God's promises? Will you see God differently?

Will you receive His promises by faith? Will you wait for His timing, resisting the desire to waver? Allow God's promises to take hold of your life and watch what He will do. He will perform miracles in your life.

Say YES to a Prosperous Soul

"Beloved, I pray that you may prosper in all things and be in health, just as your soul prospers." (3 John 1:2, NKJV)

God has distinguished man from all other creation by giving us the ability through our spirit to perceive spiritual matters and respond to spiritual stimuli. We are made up of three different areas: spirit, soul and body.

Our spirit allows us to have continual communication with the Lord and the power to interact with God--giving, receiving, responding and desiring intimate relationship with Him. There are over 1000 references in Scripture to the Spirit giving us direction in our lives.

Our soul is the seat of our mind, will, emotions, and personality. This is the battleground with the enemy. This is the place where we work out our salvation with fear and trembling.

Our body is an instrument that is used for righteousness or unrighteousness (Romans 6:12-14).

Whatever we allow to control us will determine what our body does. How is your soul prospering? What is the condition of your soul?

What Season is Your Soul In?

Is it winter? I live in Canada. We experience four seasons and the winter season is my least favourite. Inevitably, we face various weather patterns and mostly cold temperatures. "White stuff" (snow) covers the ground and nothing seems to grow. Many things lay dormant in winter.

Is it spring? Every spring, birds begin to sing, flowers begin to bud and the ground becomes moist with the thawing of the snow. It's a time to plant and sow seed.

The climate of new things, new ideas, new growth, freshness, faith, hope and expectations is fostered.

Is it summer? Summer is a wonderful time of year, a time for leisure and rest. It also is a time of waiting and enduring hot days. Things are growing but not always as fast as we like.

Is it fall? In the natural, the harvest season is the focal point for any farmer. Everything we do during the other seasons is because we want to see fruit come at the end. It can be said that the other seasons find the purpose of their existence in the harvest. These are moments when we begin to see the fruit of our labour and dreams fulfilled. Harvest time is always a season of thankfulness.

Whatever season we are in, we need to be careful what we are sowing into our lives. What we sow

- will make us STRONG or WEAK IN THOUGHT;
- will make us STRONG or WEAK IN ACTION;
- will make us STRONG or WEAK IN OUR CHOICES.

In each of these areas, what happens will depend upon the condition of our soul.

We need to develop a biblical soul posture.

The Word of God has many descriptions of attitudes we need to carry in our lives. Here are just a few:

Thirsting - Psalms 63
Bowed - Psalms 44:25
Broken - Psalms 119:20
Satisfied - Psalms 63:5
Fainting - Psalms 119:81
Boasting - Psalms 34:2
Generous - Proverbs 11:25
Guarded - Proverbs 21:23
Trusting - Psalms 57:1

Longing - Psalms 84:2
Hungry - Psalms 107:9
Clinging - Psalms 119:25
Melting - Psalms 119:28
Waiting - Psalms 33:19
Panting - Psalms 42
Diligent - Proverbs13:4
Anchored - Hebrews 6:19

"Losing the soul for the sake of the Lord is not letting one's soul be gratified in its lustful demands and delights." (Watchman Nee)[1]

What Weakens Your Soul?

"The eye is not satisfied with seeing, nor the ear filled with hearing." (Ecclesiastes 1:8, NKJV)

In Genesis 4, the Lord has a conversation with Cain. Cain had brought a sub-par offering to the Lord and it wasn't accepted.

Cain didn't know it but his soul was being weakened and was slowly eroding. God wants our best and when we don't present our best there are consequences.

There are 5 things that can cause our soul to weaken:

1. Not Giving Your Best to the Lord

Are you grateful for what God has done in your life?

A flourishing soul can be weakened with the wrong approach to the Lord. Cain didn't put his best before the Lord and God wanted more from him. This doesn't get discussed much in our grace-centered approach to Christianity, but God wants our best. At times, He expects more from our lives, particularly from those who know better. Cain knew what was expected but he chose to tip God rather than give Him his best. God was looking at the heart rather than the behaviour. Cain's heart was far away from God's best.

2. Not Dealing with Your Emotions

What happens when things don't go the way you want them to? When you don't get what you want? Do you allow your life to be directed by your feelings? Anger began to take hold of Cain and began to take control of his emotions. He allowed comparison to create a wedge between him and his brother Abel.

He began to let anger become an offense that then became a stronghold in his thinking.

3. Allowing Negative Attitudes to take Hold

Your attitudes toward God, church, friendships and authority will be reflected in your outward appearance and body language. The Lord addressed this in Cain's life. He noticed Cain's countenance and addressed how that actually indicated something happening deeper in his heart. How is your countenance? Is it reflecting what is happening internally? When we look at giving God our best, we must also be aware of our countenance.

4. Not Doing What You Know to be Right

It may be that you're not doing anything wrong, but are you doing what you know to be right? Are your ears turned away from truth? Are you at the place you know you should be at?

5. Not Conquering the Sin at your Door

God has given us everything we need to live godly and righteously. He desires that we learn to conquer the sin that can so easily come into our lives. He wants us to master the things that try to take us away from Him. He wants us to rely on Him to assist us in the journey. Cain was not willing to take the steps necessary to do this and he paid a stiff price for allowing these areas to spiral out of control.

When we are faced with the challenges that the enemy brings to our soul, I think there are specific steps we can take to avoid the mistakes that Cain made.

Speak to Your Soul

Why are you cast down, O my soul? And why are you disquieted within me? Hope in God, for I shall yet praise Him for the help of His countenance. ... Why are you cast down, O my soul? And why are you disquieted within me? Hope in God; for I shall yet praise Him, The help of my countenance and my God. (Psalm 42:5,11, NKJV)

David spoke to his soul. We need to learn how to encourage ourselves in the Lord. Prophecy to yourself, speak God's Word over your life each day, and allow the power of confession to be present in your daily routine. Whenever we are in the midst of the battle and facing temptation, we can learn to speak life into our souls and move away from negative places of thinking and action.

"So David and his men came to the city, and there it was, burned with fire; and their wives, their sons, and their daughters had been taken captive. Then David and the people who were with him lifted up their voices and wept,

until they had no more power to weep. And David's two wives, Ahinoam the Jezreelitess, and Abigail the widow of Nabal the Carmelite, had been taken captive. Now David was greatly distressed, for the people spoke of stoning him, because the soul of all the people was grieved, every man for his sons and his daughters. But David strengthened himself in the LORD his God." (1 Samuel 30:3-6, NKJV)

We must learn to build ourselves up in our most holy faith, praying in the Holy Spirit and keeping ourselves in the love of God.

"But you, beloved, building yourselves up on your most holy faith, praying in the Holy Spirit, keep yourselves in the love of God, looking for the mercy of our Lord Jesus Christ unto eternal life." (Jude 20-21, NKJV)

Feed Your Soul

"Trust in the Lord and do good, feed on His faithfulness. Delight yourself in the Lord and He will give you the desires of your heart." (Psalm 37:4-5, NKJV)

There are certain foods that immediately produce energy in your body when they are consumed. Likewise, when you begin to digest and feed on God's faithfulness, it can bring energy to your soul.

Your testimony of what God has done in your life—how He delivered you, redeemed you and brought good things to pass in your journey—is a declaration of God's faithfulness in your life. The enemy wants to steal and destroy your testimony! Revelation 12:11 says, "And they overcame him by the blood of the Lamb and by the word of their testimony, and they did not love their lives to the death." Every time you declare your testimony and feed on God's faithfulness, you overcome the enemy of anxiety and fear in your life.

Educate Your Soul

How well your soul is educated becomes evident when it is tested. What you have put into your heart and mind will come out when you are under pressure. How do you respond when facing discouragement? What reflexes do you reveal when criticized? How well do you handle stress, criticism or setbacks? When you come through with grace and wisdom, it indicates that your soul has been trained and educated to handle difficult times.

"It is not good for the soul to be without knowledge." (Proverbs 19:2, NKJV)

When we fill our soul each day with God's Word and Spirit, we train our soul to respond in faith and grace. We add new knowledge on how to respond as Christ would. We grow in maturity and develop spiritual strength.

Anchor Your Soul

"So God has given both his promise and his oath. These two things are unchangeable because it is impossible for God to lie. Therefore, we who have fled to him for refuge can have great confidence as we hold to the hope that lies before us. This hope is a strong and trustworthy anchor for our souls. It leads us through the curtain into God's inner sanctuary." (Hebrews 6:18-19, NLT)

An anchored soul can see hope in the outcome. An anchored soul is a soul that places its hope and faith in God. An anchored soul has fled to *Him* for refuge and safety. An anchored soul is a soul that has confidence in the hope God provides in His promises.

An anchored soul is a soul that has entered a new realm in God believing that all things work together for good to those who love God and are called according to His purpose. (Romans 8:28).

Enlarge Your Soul

To enlarge something usually involves stretching, extending or modifying design for the purpose of improvement. God wants us to allow our souls to be enlarged and stretched.

Jabez prayed in 1 Chronicles 4:10 for God to enlarge his territory: And Jabez called on the God of Israel saying, "Oh, that You would bless me indeed, and enlarge my territory, that Your hand would be with me, and that You would keep me from evil, that I may not cause pain!" So God granted him what he requested. (NKJV)

Isaiah 54:2-3 encourages us to enlarge the places where we dwell:

Enlarge the place of your tent, and let them stretch out the curtains of your dwellings; Do not spare; lengthen your cords, and strengthen your stakes. For you shall expand to the right and to the left, and your descendants will inherit the nations, and make the desolate cities inhabited. (NKJV)

There are moments in all of our lives when we must allow our souls to be enlarged. Without that, God cannot bring us to new places or new territories. He has so much He wants for us to experience but this can only come as our souls are enlarged to have a new capacity for new capability.

Hold Your Soul Accountable

"I will praise You, for I am fearfully and wonderfully made; Marvelous are Your works, And that my soul knows very well." (Psalms 139:14, NKJV)

Each day, we need to take steps to hold our soul accountable for how we think, how we feel and the decisions we make. Challenge your soul to live a certain way, to bring your emotions in check and to think on good things.

"Finally, brethren, whatever things are true, whatever things [are] noble, whatever things [are] just, whatever things [are] pure, whatever things [are] lovely, whatever things [are] of good report, if [there is] any virtue and if [there is] anything praiseworthy--meditate on these things. The things which you learned and received and heard and saw in me, these do, and the God of peace will be with you." (Philippians 4:8-9,NKJV

Say YES to Being Shaken

"So don't turn a deaf ear to these gracious words. If those who ignored earthly warnings didn't get away with it, what will happen to us if we turn our backs on heavenly warnings? His voice that time shook the earth to its foundations; this time—he's told us this quite plainly—he'll also rock the heavens: "One last shaking, from top to bottom, stem to stern." The phrase "one last shaking" means a thorough housecleaning, getting rid of all the historical and religious junk so that the unshakable essentials stand clear and uncluttered. Do you see what we've got? An unshakable kingdom! And do you see how thankful we must be? Not only thankful, but brimming with worship, deeply reverent before God. For God is not an indifferent bystander. He's actively cleaning house, torching all that needs to burn, and he won't quit until it's all cleansed. God himself is Fire!" (Hebrews 12:26-28, MSG)

What we say YES to will dramatically begin to alter our destiny and outlook on life. There's always a lot more going on than what we are seeing or experiencing.

God is developing in each of us something that will allow us to handle the destiny and plan He has for our lives.

Isaiah 14:27 states, "For the Lord of hosts has purposed, and who will annul it? His hand is stretched out, and who will turn it back?" God has always had a plan and purpose. We need to settle in our hearts and minds that whenever God purposes things to take place, they will take place! Nothing can stop them!

We all have gone through situations and circumstances that test our faith and may even cause us to question God.

It's important in difficult times—even when what is happening seems terrible—to see and believe that God can actually be orchestrating His purposes to elevate us to another level.

The removal and shaking process is God's way of getting rid of things of less importance and retaining those things that have greater value. He knows best and He knows what we need for the journey!

"He has promised, saying, "Once again I will shake not only the earth but the heavens also." This means that all of creation will be shaken and removed, so that only unshakable things will remain. Since we are receiving a Kingdom that is unshakable, let us be thankful and please God by worshiping him with holy fear and awe. For our God is a consuming fire." (Hebrews 12:26-28, NKJV)

One of the promises that God has spoken in His Word is that He is going to shake and remove what is temporary so that what is eternal and of lasting value will remain. God wants us to say YES to being shaken! We must be willing to remove everything that will prevent us from achieving all that He has prepared for us.

"God's intent is not to shake us to break us, but to bring us to new levels of life in HIM. To break through to a higher level of life requires power, supernatural power that humans, in our own strength, are incapable of producing."
(Joey Bonifacio)[1]

God is so committed to us that He wants to remove everything that should be removed in us so that He can put into us that which will last.

Last year, my son got engaged—a very exciting time in our family. We decided to build a basement apartment to help him and his new bride save money toward a down payment for a house.

We had lived in our house for about five years and had basically an open basement. With this decision, we had to clear out our basement and evaluate what we had down there. You don't realize how in just a few short years how much stuff you can accumulate.

Here's what I found can happen with the accumulation of things in our lives. We find things that are just junk, they're taking up space. I'm really not sure how they got down there. Some things were just put down there to get them out of the way. I guess we had hoped to forget or avoid dealing with them. Some things were brought over from the previous house that should have been dealt with back then!

We also found things that we thought we would use but never did: my wife's great-grandma's old foot-stool that had a big stain on it and was missing a leg, bags with little bags inside them, a box with other little boxes in it, an old table and chair set that wasn't even ours. Can you see where this is going? These things can be sentimental in value but take up room for things that can be useful and productive.

We also found things that had outlasted their value or usefulness: old golf carts, sports equipment, luggage, old TV receivers and an old Motorola cellular flip phone. With these items we had to decide whether to give them away, get rid of them or redefine their purpose.

Is their junk in your life? Are there things you're holding on to for sentimental reasons? Are there things that you need to give away, redefine or simply get rid of?

We all have things that are taking up space in our hearts. We all have things that we are familiar with and hold as memories that we need to let go of in order to move into our future.

If we are willing to do an inventory of the rooms in our hearts and as we allow the Holy Spirit to address the things that would keep us back, we can experience great breakthrough. When we deal with the things that weigh us down, we are free to move into our divine purpose.

The Bible encourages us to remove a few things from our lives. We are encouraged to remove the leaven from our houses. Exodus 12:15 states, "On the first day you shall remove leaven from your houses" (NKJV). I'm not a baker but I do understand you only need a little leaven in dough to make it rise to a large loaf of bread.

Leaven can represent the small things in our heart that we need to be willing to remove. If we don't, they can eventually become larger issues. Little attitudes left unchecked can foster a root of bitterness or anger. Small hurts not dealt with can become wounds that harden the heart and cause us to live in deception. A little thought can become an argument, which eventually can lead to a stronghold that can keep you bound and hold you back from advancing. Many of us believe small lies. But even small lies lead to hopelessness and defeat.

Before we go any further, take a few minutes right now to ask the Lord to search your heart. See what He points out. Be honest with yourself and begin the process of downsizing and removing the junk in your life.

Let Go of a Critical Spirit

It's so easy to look at someone and make judgments about what they are doing or saying. We live in a judgmental society and, unfortunately, it has slipped into the church.

In Luke 6:42, Jesus calls us to look at our own lives and remove the plank in our eye before we address what another person is doing.

"Or how can you say to your brother, "Brother, let me remove the speck that is in your eye,' when you yourself do not see the plank that is in your own eye? Hypocrite! **First remove the plank from your own eye, and then you will see clearly to remove the speck that is in your brother's eye.***" (Luke 6:42, NKJV)*

Being judgmental and critical changes the way we see people. We can't see the best another person has to offer because our vision is clouded by hurt or offenses. We can miss a great opportunity to encourage the uniqueness of the individual and what they have to offer to others. We are called to seek out a better way, to love those who may be different. We are called to look first at our own lives before we begin to judge another.

I have a friend who makes it a policy to never speak negatively of other ministers. I applaud my friend. I think he gets the "plank principle". It is so easy to make quick judgments about people or situations when we may not know all the facts.

As the old saying goes, "Better to be thought a fool than to open your mouth and remove all doubt." In our internet blogging world, anyone can easily become a target of someone else's judgments. Let's try to not add fuel to this process.

Let Go of Disappointment

"Therefore remove sorrow from your heart." (Ecclesiastes 11:10, NKJV)

As a young Christian, I went through a number of disappointing situations that had the potential to cause deep sorrow in my heart. God encourages us to remove sorrow from our lives.

When God encourages us to remove sorrow from our hearts, He's talking about the trouble that man can inflict which causes hurt feelings leading to anger, grief and spite. This type of sorrow can invade your life quickly.

Many carry sorrow around in their heart each day— significant issues that cause heaviness, despair and even hopelessness. God wants us to remove this sorrow out of our hearts. There needs to be an intentional process of dealing with these hurts or we will be stuck on a never-ending hamster wheel going nowhere fast. One of the blessings of following Jesus is that He makes our lives rich and adds no sorrow to them.

Sorrow must be dealt with as quickly as possible or it can spiral into depression and defeat. I want to encourage you to allow the Holy Spirit access to these deep wounds so He can bring healing. Maintaining a forgiving and grateful heart is key to resolving these wounds.

In Hebrews 12:21, we are encouraged to remove anything that would get in the way: "So let us run the race that is before us and never give up. We should remove from our lives anything that would get in the way and the sin that so easily holds us back" (NLT).

Whatever is getting in the way of serving God needs to be evaluated and removed. There must be an intentional removal of these things or they will become weights that slow down and even halt our forward progress. This is a personal journey of releasing the hindrances and things that hold us back.

Shaken for a Purpose

A number of years ago, my son and I were on a mission trip in Veracruz, Mexico. Around 6:00 in the morning, our beds began to shake and the TV hanging from the ceiling began to move steadily. I woke up knowing that we were experiencing an earthquake.

I wasn't sure how well-built our hotel was, so we proceeded towards the hallway. The earthquake lasted only a few seconds but the whole building awoke from their sleep.

Paul and Silas were in dark, dungy prison in the middle of the night after being falsely accused when *"Suddenly there was a great earthquake, so that the foundations of the prison were shaken; and immediately all the doors were opened and everyone's chains were loosed." (Acts 16:26, NKJV)*

I believe that being shaken can be a very good thing. It can loose things that have a hold on us and can also awaken us to new possibilities in our lives. God wants to shake the prison doors of people's lives and loose them from the things that are binding them and keeping them back.

What doors in your life need to be opened? What about in the lives of your unsaved friends? What chains have a hold on you? On them? Paul and Silas were simply praising God and, no doubt, believing for a unique supernatural outcome. Regardless of what has a hold on us or what doors are closed, God wants to release us, open new doors and bring freedom to our lives. Will you believe God to shake open the prison doors?

Will you believe God to break the chains that are holding you or your friends? Will you say yes to being shaken?

This year can be a year of breakthrough and freedom in the lives of people who will come to know the Lord! Chains can be broken off and they can live in greater freedom than ever before.

Financial Shaking

In our world there is a shaking going on in regards to finances. Countries are defaulting on their loans, national debt is rising and people are feeling the pressure from job losses, downsizing, rising food prices, etc. However, God speaks very clearly in His Word that He will shake the heavens and the earth and supernaturally bring in silver and gold into the house of God.

"For this is what the LORD of Heaven's Armies says: In just a little while I will again shake the heavens and the earth, the oceans and the dry land. I will shake all the nations, and **the treasures of all the nations will be brought to this Temple***. I will fill this place with glory, says the LORD of Heaven's Armies. The silver is mine, and the gold is mine, says the LORD of Heaven's Armies. The future glory of this Temple will be greater than its past glory, says the LORD of Heaven's Armies. And in this place I will bring peace. I, the LORD of Heaven's Armies, have spoken!" (Haggai 2:6-9, NLT)*

God wants us to be responsible with our finances but there are clearly times when we need a breakthrough. Churches are looking to expand and do more kingdom initiatives, all which will take money to accomplish. Each individual and church will need to believe for supernatural breakthrough, breakthrough that can only come through God sovereignly shaking the heavens and releasing financial provision. It's the heart of God to want to bless His people!

In this past year I have heard so many stories of God's provision. I personally know of churches that have seen the blessing of God being poured out in their communities. One church received a cheque from a man for $100,000 and then their Prime Minister called and gave them another $50,000. You know it's a miracle when the government is giving you money! Two other churches received miracle offerings of $98,000 and $158,000. I've watched churches receive land for a dollar, had buildings given to them and had supernatural provision come from the most unlikely sources.

In my own life, I have watched as I have faithfully tithed, God has supernaturally shaken the heavens and provided needed resources at critical junctures in my journey.

It's a promise of God that, if we believe Him, He will shake the heavens and the earth on our behalf. He wants to fill your temple and the house of God.

Each generation desires and believes for a great outpouring and revival to take place. In my lifetime, there have been a number of waves where the Holy Spirit broke into the church and began to move.

People received Jesus into their hearts and many were filled with the Holy Spirit and became established in the Word of God.

*"And when they had prayed, the place where they were assembled together was shaken; and they were **all filled with the Holy Spirit**, and **they spoke the word of God with boldness**." (Acts 4:31, NKJV)*

Today, more than at any time, there is a growing sense of hopelessness among the younger generation.

Young people are confused about their identity and purpose. People have placed their trust in things rather than in the absolutes of God's unchanging Word. These things don't provide security and deep inner satisfaction.

The only person that can do that is Jesus Christ living in our hearts.

As we say YES to being shaken, we are inviting God to begin to shake our lives for service and purpose, to be His voice and hands to a hurting and confused world. He wants to fill each of us with His power and Spirit whereby we can speak life through His Word to people in need. I believe that in the coming days, we are going to see a move of the Holy Spirit like we have never seen before.

Say YES to the Good Fight

*"Timothy, my son, I give you this instruction in keeping with the prophecies once made about you, so that by following them you may **fight the good fight**, holding on to faith and a good conscience. Some have rejected these and so have shipwrecked their faith." (1 Timothy 1:18-20, NKJV)*

*"**Fight the good fight of faith**, lay hold on eternal life, to which you were also called and have confessed the good confession in the presence of many witnesses." (1 Timothy 6:12, NKJV)*

"Leave no unguarded place, no weakness of soul; take every virtue, every grace, and fortify the whole from strength to strength; go on, wrestle and fight and pray, tread all the powers of darkness down and win the well-fought day." (John Wesley)[1]

Anytime we step out in faith and begin to walk with God, we become a target for the enemy. He wants to beat us down and discourage us. He wants to try to stop the purposes of God in our lives. The enemy has set a plot and laid a siege for our lives. He has openly declared war on our fundamental beliefs and what we hold as precious.

His goal is to destroy our ability to trust God and say YES to His promises. He wants to shipwreck our faith.

In an attempt to take a church or a Christian, a siege is ensued over a period of time so that the enemy can isolate, weaken and destroy the defenses of his target. The definition of a siege is: to hem in, to cause distress, to cramp or confine, to harass and torment inciting an outward conflict or battle.[2] The enemy targets a number of areas in our lives and he will do it over a prolonged period of time.

These areas include our relationship with God, our attitude toward leadership, our inner thoughts, our faith and zeal and our relationship with other people.

Our Relationship with God

Everything we do in relation to developing our walk with God will come under attack. When we spend time each day meeting the Lord in our devotions, it brings strength and stamina to our lives as we face whatever comes our way.

The enemy does not want us to succeed in our relationship with God. *He wants to cramp our style or hinder our connection with God.* When we allow the enemy to distract us from meeting God daily, we lose our ability to fight and pull down the lies that he consistently tries to assault us with.

Each of us needs to carve out our time to make spending time with Jesus a priority. Grab a cup of coffee or tea, get your Bible and notebook, put on some good music and spend a few minutes connecting with the One who loves you more than you can imagine.

You will be amazed at what He will speak to you.

Our Attitude towards Leadership

The enemy would want nothing more than for each of us to carry around leadership wounds that would limit us from enjoying our purpose and place. God has ordained authority and He has encouraged us to develop relationships with those in authority as they nurture and care for our lives.

Leaders carry a large responsibility as they serve the people of God. There are many great leaders who go above and beyond the call of duty to see people experience the best God has to offer. Our lives are changed and transformed by the gospel and the leadership God has placed in our lives.

We need to have a healthy respect and honour for these great men and women of God. However, leaders are human and can make mistakes, say things that aren't what we think are best to say and even do things that don't represent what God would have intended. We can be affected by their poor choices. They may cause wounds and hurts that affect us deeply, misunderstandings that can take the wind out of our sails. The enemy can easily begin to sow seeds of disappointment, offense and bitterness in our lives and we need to be on guard against this.

We must resist the opportunity to react in immaturity. Rather, we should respond with the maturity that comes from Christ and His Word. The enemy wants to lay siege to our ability to trust and honour leaders. We need to allow God's grace to be applied to leaders through forgiveness.

Everyone has leaders in their lives. Take a few moments today and thank God for them, bless them and look for ways to serve them as they lay down their lives for God's kingdom.

You will never be disappointed when your motive is pure and right before the Lord.

Our Inner Thoughts

Our society bombards us with many ungodly images. We are inundated with so many sensory images that we have become desensitized to what is right and wrong. Holiness and discretion aren't even words that cross many people's vocabulary anymore.

The enemy has and continues to lay siege against our minds, seeking to conform us to the world's image and attitude. Now more than ever we need to fight and bring into subjection any thought that is not from God.

God is just as concerned about our inner thoughts as our outer actions. Any thought that doesn't line up with His thoughts must be considered a lie and pulled down. We must bring our soul into submission to the Spirit of God within.

"You can't afford to have thoughts in your mind that don't line up with the thoughts in His mind." (Bill Johnson)[3]

Take a few minutes to evaluate your intake. What are you listening to or watching? What would Jesus want you to remove from your life?

What have you become desensitized to? This could be a moment of liberation and release in your life. Focusing on the right things always produces good results.

Our Faith and Zeal

Every single person has a calling. God has a specific purpose for each of us to fulfill. When we start our journey, there is a tremendous amount of excitement and enthusiasm for what lies ahead. We anticipate great things to take place and very little opposition. The enemy does not want us to succeed so he begins to sow seeds of discouragement and disappointment in our hearts. If left unchecked, we can become apathetic and no longer zealous for the things of God.

We can also become comfortable and captivated by blessing and success. We can become complacent and captivated by pleasure and security. The enemy pressures us to redefine and remove our underlying convictions.

Each of us must determine that we will pursue the call of God on our lives and live with purpose in all we do. We can't allow the enemy to lull us to sleep. We must be willing to stay activated to the call and purpose God has for our lives.

"The enemy's tactics seem to be as follows. He will first of all oppose our breaking through to the place of real, living faith, by all means in his power. He detests the prayer of faith, for it is an authoritative 'notice to quit.' He does not so much mind rambling, carnal prayers, for they do not hurt him much.... However, once we attain to a real faith, all the forces of hell are impotent to annul it." (Eileen Crossman)[4]

When you begin the journey of faith, the enemy of your soul will seek to sow a seed of unbelief in your heart and cause you to no longer take faith steps or make character changes. The devil will tempt you to shift into maintenance mode. We begin to use phrases like, "I've tried that and it didn't work!" or "Maybe another day!" or "I wish I could but..."

Now that I have served Jesus for over 30 years, I look back on my journey and am amazed at the adventure it has been.

There have been many twists and turns—some great, some bad and some just pure ugly! As I reflect, I wouldn't change anything. Each stage of the journey has required steps of faith, a willingness to accept a new adventure and a willingness to trust in a good God who has all things under His control.

Throughout the years, the enemy has been right there trying to sow seeds of doubt and unbelief, trying to remove the zeal and energy required to stand in faith. Yet, in all of this, he hasn't won. I'm more excited today than when I was in my late teens.

My life is thriving—all because I would not let the enemy steal my faith or weaken my soul.

What about you? Have you grown weary or discouraged?

"Spiritual maturity—or spiritual formation—is defined at its core not by being busy with a lot of Christian activities, or knowing a lot about the Bible, or piling up spiritual accomplishments. The Pharisees did all of these things, and Jesus said they were the least fruitful of anybody. To grow in authentic Biblical love, joy, peace and patience— that's the center of the target!"[5] Author Unknown

Take a moment and breathe deeply. Decide to take a fresh step of faith in your journey. Why not reach out to someone at church, in your neighbourhood or at work; get in a Bible study group; or spend some time with someone in need and watch what God will begin to do in your heart! A new faith and excitement will begin to flood your soul.

Our Relationship with Others

Each day, our lives are filled with interactions with humanity. These interactions can be wonderful moments of engagement that lead to tremendous connection, love and laughter. However, they can also be times of disconnection that lead to hurt, offense and pain.

Our interactions with one another can be target points where the enemy wants to bring discord and destruction. They are target points where incredible hurt and pain can take place and where we experience loss of connection and purpose.

If you have a relationship where this has happened, search your heart to see what can be done. Are there steps you can take to repair and rebuild those connections?

Send a card or note to let the person know you're thinking about or praying for them. Don't give the enemy opportunity to sow discord in your heart but allow the Holy Spirit to spread God's love in your life. Choose daily to forgive and release those who have hurt you.

1 Peter 2:23 declares of Jesus, "He did not retaliate when he was insulted, nor threaten revenge when he suffered. He left his case in the hands of God, who always judges fairly." NLT Give your relationships into the hand of the One who knows how to judge fairly. He is faithful to adjust and correct things that are out of order when we place our trust Him.

Our Convictions and Values

"There is no noble task ever accomplished that does not have some significant adversity before the final goal." (Rick Johnston)[6]

Our society has an agenda to shape and mold our convictions and values. The Scripture admonishes us to not let this happen! If we are not careful, our once-strong convictions will slowly begin to wane and grow lukewarm. Things we didn't tolerate five years ago, we now allow. We need to wake up to the fact that the enemy has laid siege on our lives.

"Don't become so well-adjusted to your culture that you fit into it without even thinking. Instead, fix your attention on God. You'll be changed from the inside out. Readily recognize what he wants from you, and quickly respond to it. Unlike the culture around you, always dragging you down to its level of immaturity, God brings the best out of you, develops well-formed maturity in you." (Romans 12:2, MSG)

"Don't copy the behavior and customs of this world, but let God transform you into a new person by changing the way you think. Then you will learn to know God's will for you, which is good and pleasing and perfect." (Romans 12:2, NLT)

"Do not allow this world to mold you in its own image. Instead, be transformed from the inside out by renewing your mind. As a result, you will be able to discern what God wills and whatever God finds good, pleasing, and complete." (Romans 12:2, Voice)

Many of us have allowed the society we live in to shape our thinking to the point that the Bible has become somewhat irrelevant. We have allowed our worldview to be shaped by philosophies and worldly thinking.

We have become insensitive to what the world calls right, even when God clearly states is wrong. We have allowed ourselves to be marked by media, sports and pleasure rather than standing out in these places as beacons of light declaring a better way.

We need to get back to the Word as the standard by which we live and evaluate our lives. When we do this, we will be able to stand strong and be anchored to truths that have stood the test of time.

We can become a group of people who are highly skilled with supernatural gift and godly character that will model a new and better way for a hopeless, worn out generation to follow.

The enemy wants to target us in our thinking and, as we will see later, the end is confusion, chaos and destruction if we give into this unbiblical worldview.

The Armour of God

Every believer more than ever needs to intentionally put on the armour of God each day! It is a significant way to protect and defend ourselves from the attacks of the enemy. If we are going to say YES to the good fight of faith then we must put on the whole Armour of God.

I am indebted to Dr. Wendell Smith and Dr. Larry Lea for their teaching on prayer and many of the tools they have laid out for us. One of the components that I added to my life over 25 years ago was putting on the armour of God on a daily basis. It has served as a means of protection, a reminder of the battle we are in and the ultimate victory we have when we embrace the gospel truths covered in the Apostle Paul's description.

*"Therefore take up the whole armour of God, that you may be able to withstand in the evil day, and having done all, to stand. Stand therefore, having **girded your waist with truth**, having put on **the breastplate of righteousness**,*

and having shod your **feet with the preparation of the gospel of peace**; above all, taking the **shield of faith** with which you will be able to quench all the fiery darts of the wicked one. Put on **salvation as your helmet**, and take the sword of the Spirit, which is the word of God. **Pray in the Spirit** at all times and on every occasion. Stay alert and be persistent in your prayers for all believers everywhere." (Ephesians 6:13-18, NKJV)

Let's look at each of these individually.

The Belt of Truth

We are encouraged to gird ourselves with truth—to surround ourselves with it. Truth is like a belt that keeps everything in place and leaves nothing exposed. The adversary can successfully assail those with no consistent intake of truth. Absolute biblical truth must be the bedrock of a person's life.

The enemy will consistently speak lies into our lives and we need to daily spend time in the Word of God, allowing the Holy Spirit access to shape our thoughts according to His truth. This requires a willingness to surrender beliefs and opinions that are not consistent with God's Word.

Our goal each day should be to make the soul sincere, firm, constant and always on its guard. Truth allows us to make that happen. Take a moment and let truth capture your heart and mind today. God loves you! God accepts you! God has a great plan for your life! God wants your best! God has set you in a good place! God is for you and not against you! God is working all things for your good!

The Breastplate of Righteousness

"Guard your heart; for out of it flows the issues of life." (Proverbs 4:23)

Every person will have to deal with actions done to them that have caused hurt, pain and the potential for inner turmoil. We also will face the onslaught of various temptations throughout week.

The enemy is seeking to attack your inner life, bringing unforgiveness, bitterness, anxiety, shame and pain.

We need to daily put on the breastplate of righteousness to defend against the flaming arrows sent to injure and wound. These flaming missiles from the enemy are nothing more than smoldering lies, burning accusations and fiery temptations that bombard our minds and attack our hearts. I want to encourage you to let the righteousness of Christ guard your heart. Let forgiveness be a part of each day, forgive yourself and forgive others. Let offenses slide off your back like water off a duck's back. Determine to hold no grudges. Remove the root of bitterness.

Boots of Peace

Many times we underestimate the wear and tear on our feet as we go about our day. The price of a good pair of shoes can go a long way toward comfort and peace.

The Roman army would invest quite a lot in a soldier's boots because they recognized that a soldier would be on their feet each day and in terrain that required strong craftsmanship. When the army was under attack, they needed to know their footwork would be secure and strong to hold their positions. The Apostle Paul recognized this and applied this to the believer's life by encouraging them to put on the boots of the gospel of peace.

Isaiah 32:17-18 states, "The work of righteousness will be peace, and the effect of righteousness, quietness and assurance forever. My people will dwell in a peaceful habitation, in secure dwellings, and in quiet resting places."

When trouble is all around us, we need to stand in peace. When everything around us seems to crumble, we need to stand in peace. In the midst of difficulty, each of us can know a peace that passes understanding.

When the enemy begins to make an assault on our faith, standing in a position of peace will go a long way toward winning the victory.

In Ephesians 4:27, the amplified version says, "Leave no such room or foothold for the devil, give no opportunity to him." The gospel has provided all that we need to live a successful and godly life.

As believers, we cannot give the devil a foothold. We cannot give him room in our lives to influence us in any way. God's desire is to "redeem our soul in peace from the battle that was against us, for there were many against us" (Psalms 55:18). God promises us in Isaiah 26:3 that "He will keep him in perfect peace, whose mind is stayed on You, because he trusts in You." As we focus on God, He will give us peace from the battles against us.

How is your footing? How are your boots? Are you standing in peace? Are you accessing the good news of the gospel? Stand in peace and watch what God will do in your battle. His peace will keep you in the midst of the storm. Take a moment, close your eyes and focus upon Jesus. Let Him speak peace into your heart and mind.

Shield of Faith

"Above all, taking the shield of faith with which you will be able to quench all the fiery darts of the wicked one." (Ephesians 6:16, NKJV)

In the remake of *Robin Hood* with Russel Crowe, there is a scene in which they are advancing against a fortified city.

They all take their shields and put them together to create an impenetrable barrier. This allows them to slowly move towards the doors and protects them against the archer's arrows. As a result, they eventually penetrate the doors and break through the city.

"A shield was usually made of light-wood or a rim of brass, and covered with several folds or thicknesses of stout hide, which was preserved by frequent anointing with oil. It was generally held by the left arm, and was secured by straps through which the arm passed. The outer surface of the shield was made more or less rounded from the center to the edge and was polished smooth or anointed with oil, so that arrows or darts would rebound off of it. After a battle, each shield would be rubbed with oil, cleaned from battle and re-hung, ready for another battle." (International Standard Bible Dictionary)[7]

The rubbing of oil was a crucial part for the **longevity of the shield**. Without the regular rubbing of oil, the shield would become hard and brittle and break, allowing the archers arrow to penetrate.

When the Holy Spirit is allowed to operate in our lives each day, the enemy's arrows can't penetrate our defenses. Without the daily presence of God flowing through our lives, our minds begin to grow dry and brittle. Bitterness, anger and defeat begin to take hold of our thinking. Every thought must be brought under the anointing of God's Word.

"Take up" is a command to be ready, be alert for anything the enemy will throw at you. *"Faith here is made to occupy a more important place than either of the other Christian graces. It protects all, and is indispensable to the security of all. The shield was an ingenious device by which blows and arrows might be parried off, and the whole body defended. It could be made to protect the head, or the*

heart, or thrown behind to meet an attack there. As long as the soldier had his shield, he felt secure; and as long as a Christian has faith, he is safe. It comes to his aid in every attack that is made on him, no matter from what quarter; it is the defense and guardian of every other Christian grace; and it secures the protection which the Christian needs in the whole of the spiritual war." (Author Unknown)

How is your faith? Are you building yourself up in your most holy faith? What steps are you taking each day to add to your faith (Jude 20)? Is your shield a little brittle or hard (2 Peter 1:5-9)? Have you allowed the oil of God's presence to touch your shield lately?

Take a moment and open your faith to a fresh touch of oil from heaven. Let the Holy Spirit anoint you today for the journey. Spend time with Him. He wants to touch you and minister to you.

Helmet of Salvation

The helmet was a cap made of thick leather, or brass, fitted to the head, and was usually crowned with a plume, or crest, as an ornament, its use was to guard the head from a blow by a sword, or war-club, or battle-axe. When we place our hope in God and the salvation He offers we place a helmet on our minds that will preserve us in the day of battle and spiritual conflict.

"The helmet defended the head, a vital part; and so the hope of salvation will defend the soul, and keep it from the blows of the enemy. A soldier would not fight well without a hope of victory". (International Standard Bible Dictionary)[8]

*"For though we walk in the flesh, we do not war according to the flesh. For the weapons of our warfare are not carnal but mighty in God for pulling down **strongholds**, casting down **arguments** and every **high thing** that exalts itself against the knowledge of God, bringing every **thought** into*

captivity to the obedience of Christ." (2 Peter 1:5-9, NKJV)

Destructive thinking is a process. Did you know that an unchecked thought has the potential to engulf your mind? This passage teaches us four progressive levels of thinking that we must give over to God.

It begins with a thought such as, "I can't do this" or "I'm not loved". When you allow a *single thought* like one of these to begin in your mind, a process begins that, when left unchecked, creates a starting point toward a satanic stronghold gaining ground in your life. This then leads to *higher thoughts* that preoccupy your mind and begin to lead to deeper and darker reasoning in your mind. Once this cycle has started and you don't take authority and dismiss these thoughts, they quickly become a line of *arguments* that you talk yourself into believing. You can become unable to be swayed or convinced that you are wrong.

The inevitable conclusion to this is that a *stronghold* takes place and you now have given the devil an opportunity to operate in our life. Lust can take hold or fear becomes a way of life; anxiety enters your heart to stay; offense has set in and you now look to seek revenge or exact justice.

"A brother offended is harder to win than a strong city, and contentions are like the bars of a castle." (Proverbs 18:19, NKJV)

"Any area of your life not glistening with hope is believing a lie." (Francis Frangipane)[9]

Every believer needs to put on love. The love of God will bring a deep security in your soul and, once that is in place, peace will be allowed to rule in your heart and mind.

The Apostle Paul admonishes us to, "above all these things put on love, which is the bond of perfection. And let the peace of God rule in your hearts" (Colossians 3:14-15, NKJV). Every negative thought must be stopped before it can take hold in our hearts and minds.

If you are dealing with a stronghold issue, ask the Lord to direct you to the lie that you are holding on to. Believe God and renounce this from your life. Ask Him to evict the enemy from that strong place. Replace that thought with

the truth of God's Word. Determine to put on the helmet of salvation and renew your mind in peace. Allow specific thoughts to be taken captive and stop the process of destructive strongholds being set up in your life. Instead, allow the love and peace of God to become a stronghold of protection and security.

Sword of the Spirit

Perhaps the greatest way to say yes to the good fight of faith is to take up the sword of the Spirit.

I believe when the Apostle Paul was encouraging us to "take up", he was saying that we need to allow the living Word to take hold of us. Hebrews chapter 4 describes the Word of God as, "quick and powerful, active and living, dividing between soul and spirit joints and marrow, discerning the very thoughts and intents of the heart of man."

God's Word is a weapon that He gives to every believer. It is more than written words on a page, it is a living, prophetic word given by the Holy Spirit for us to wage war with. God has many thoughts that He thinks towards you. Those thoughts become His words to strengthen and build your faith. The Holy Spirit takes these prophetic words and wants to wield, to exercise power and authority as a dominating effective weapon against the lies of the enemy set against us.

"For a sword take the words that the Spirit gives from God." (Ephesians 6:17, NEB)

"The sword that the Spirit wields, which is the Word of God." (Ephesians 6:17, MSG)

God has a "now" word for our lives, a living active word that will do damage to the kingdom of darkness and rescue people from the enemy's grip. It is a word of promise that He wants you to fight with, the prophetic word given by the Lord to help dominate and effectively wage battle against the enemies we face.

"Prophecy is given to dislodge hindrances in people's lives by proclaiming the possible into their lives." (Graham Cooke)[10]

Prophecy brings hope and helps people break free from the status quo of their present situation. It will advance a person into a place they have not been before. It reminds the devil of our future and reminds him of his end. It reminds him that we are children of destiny and purpose and that the gates of hell will not hold us back. It reminds him that, regardless of our situation, we will win.

Recently, as I was ministering at a church, I began to speak over one particular woman that God was her healer, God was her deliverer, that this was not unto death and that her testimony would be a starting point for miracles to take place in the house of the Lord. After I stopped, the pastor asked the lady if he could share her story. She had just been diagnosed with cancer.

I believe God spoke to her heart to encourage and give her a sword of the Spirit to begin to use to dominate and exercise authority over her sickness and situation. God's will is for her to be healed and set free.

What about you, friend? Do you have a promise from God?

Do you have a living Word that can become your active sword for the battle you're facing today? Why not ask the Lord to quicken something to your heart and mind. Ask Him to make His word come alive to you.

God so clearly wants to speak to your life for the journey, to engage with you in the battle and to stand with you watching you beat back the forces of darkness.

Praying in the Spirit

Prayer has always been a struggle for me. It's not that I don't pray—I do. But it can so easily turn into an empty form or method with no life in it.

Matthew 6:6-10 in the Message version speaks to me about how we need to approach prayer:

Here's what I want you to do: Find a quiet, secluded place so you won't be tempted to role-play before God. Just be there as simply and honestly as you can manage. The focus will shift from you to God, and you will begin to sense His grace. The world is full of so-called prayer warriors who are prayer-ignorant.

They're full of formulas and programs and advice, peddling techniques for getting what you want from God. Don't fall for that nonsense. This is your Father you are dealing with, and He knows better than you what you need. With a God like this loving you, you can pray very simply.

Did you catch that? Find a quiet, secluded place, a place where there are no interruptions, no texts or emails—just you and God. Then come without any masks or games. No role-playing. Just to be yourself, simple and honest.

This so reverberates in my heart—a secluded place where you can let it all come out, your fears, your pain, your joys, your questions, your concerns and your gratefulness.

I've found the times that I get serious about seeking the Lord, coming honestly before Him, the focus shifts from me to a great God. He shows me that He is a faithful God who is willing and able to help in my time of need or battle. He's a faithful God who fulfills all of His promises. He's a faithful God who supplies everything I need for the journey. He's a faithful God who heals and touches me, a faithful God who brings fresh perspective on what this journey is all about.

He reminds me time and time again that *He* is in control. He's a God who pours out His grace to anyone who asks. His grace washes over my sin-stained heart and mind. His grace enables me to fight the good fight once again. His grace lets me know I'm not alone and not forgotten.

"Without relationship, prayer becomes mere performance. Prayer is from the heart and Spirit. When the heart is on fire with God himself, then prayer is on fire. Prayer must be filled with the thoughts of God, words of God and passion for God. Prayer is the contact of a living soul with a living God." (E.M. Bounds)[11]

Prayer is a powerful weapon in the life of a believer. Prayer is not a formula or program. It is a man or woman of God connecting with a great God. It is crying out in your time of need and believing that God will answer.

"Prayer is the key that unlocks all the storehouses of God's infinite grace and power. All that God is, and has, is at the disposal of prayer. Prayer can do anything that God can do, and as God can do anything, prayer is omnipotent." (EM Bounds)[11]

As the Apostle Paul is closing his discourse on the armour of God, he adds this thought, admonition and command in Ephesians 6:16: "Pray in the Spirit at all times and on every occasion. Stay alert and be persistent in your prayers for all believers everywhere."

The enemy does not want us to pray in the Spirit. It's a language he can't understand. It's a language of warfare; it's a language of faith; it's a language that only the Godhead can understand. There are moments when we don't know how to pray. We are encouraged to pray in our prayer language, to pray in tongues. The Holy Spirit knows what we need and what battles we are facing. Let Him take over.

"Likewise the Spirit also helps in our weaknesses. For we do not know what we should pray for as we ought, but the Spirit Himself makes intercession for us with groanings which cannot be uttered. Now He who searches the hearts knows what the mind of the Spirit is, because He makes intercession for the saints according to the will of God." (Romans 8:26-27, NKJV)

We need to engage ourselves in the business of praying in the Spirit as often as we remember. It builds our faith and it connects us to a heavenly resource accessible at any time. Praying in the spirit energizes our lives in a way that nothing else will.

"Mark well this law of the Kingdom, the Holy Spirit uses prayer to work and shape our lives." (E.M. Bounds)[11]

Say YES to Your Place

"By faith Abraham obeyed when he was called to go out to the place which he would receive as an inheritance. And he went out, not knowing where he was going." (Hebrews 11:8, NKJV)

Many times while navigating the journey in Christ, we can lose sight of the real meaning and purpose of life. God's intention is to get us to a place in Him where our hearts are taken captive by His promises. The places where God turns up in our lives become places of change. When we say YES to God's place in our lives, we begin to experience the destiny and purpose for which we were created.

Faith and Obedience

*"By **faith** Abraham **obeyed** when he was called to go out to the place which he would receive as an inheritance. **And he went out, not knowing where he was going.**" (Hebrews 11:8, NKJV)*

In Hebrews 11, it says that Abraham was called to go out to the place that he would receive as his inheritance without really knowing where he was going. In Genesis, Joseph had great dreams about his future but found himself in a place which, to the mind's eye, seemed to contradict those dreams. We need faith, trust and obedience because the journey isn't always perfectly outlined nor the destination clear. Many times, where you find yourself may be confusing or make no sense at all. We must be ready and willing to embrace the place we find ourselves in and allow God to work in and through us. We need to remember that God is preparing us for something great. He is preparing us to receive our inheritance.

There are places that God wants to take us into. There are places we need to go through in order to get to the places God wants to take us into. There are places we need to establish in our lives that will help us get through the places we're going through so we can get to the places God wants to take us to.

Prayer

Every believer must establish places in their life that will help them walk into their destiny. Jesus stands at the door of your heart and wants to come in and fellowship with you. Inviting Jesus into the place of your heart is crucial to beginning the journey.

"It is given to every man to live in two worlds this world of space and time, and the world of eternal things. Our danger is to become so involved in this world that we forget the other...turn aside, if only a moment and enter God's presence. Every man carries with him his own secret place but so many forget to enter it." (Leonard Ravenhill)[1]

The secret place of prayer is essential to navigating the places in which we'll find ourselves.

When I was a teenager, I was involved in drugs and alcohol. On one particular night, I got into a fight and someone pointed a gun at my head. At that moment, my mom was at a prayer meeting, praying for her boys to come home to Christ. That night, in the place of prayer, my mom was able to break through and heaven began to move. The next night, I gave my heart to Jesus and have never turned back. My life was forever changed.

God wants us to sense His grace working in our lives regardless of our circumstances or situation. Prayer can shift atmospheres and move mountains in your life. Prayer can establish a generation of champions. Prayer can heal the sick and break open chains of those who are bound.

Holiness

One day, while Moses was going about his everyday life, he saw a bush burning supernaturally in the desert. As he came nearer, God said, "Do not draw near this place. Take your sandals off your feet, for the place where you stand is holy ground" (Exodus 3:5).

As we place Christ at the center of our lives, we must come to a place of holiness. God wants to touch every part of our lives. He loves us enough to accept us as we are but also loves us too much to let us stay that way. He desires for us to change and be transformed. He wants His presence to touch how we walk, how we act, how we think and how we speak.

Surrender

God has places He wants us to establish in our lives, not because it is always convenient or comfortable but because, in the long run, it is beneficial and necessary.

One of the benefits of reading the Bible is that we get to see the lessons that heroes of faith learned and the trials that they went through. We can see how they handled defeat, trials and pressures. We, at times, can see what God was actually doing behind the scenes and know that He always has our best interests at heart. By reading the Scripture, we gain understanding and knowledge as we walk through our own difficulties and trials.

The following Scriptures indicate that the place of surrender is a specific place that believers need to walk through"

"And they came to the place which God had told him of; and Abraham built an altar there, and laid the wood in order, and bound Isaac his son, and laid him on the altar upon the wood. (Genesis 22:9, NKJV)

"Then they came to a place which was named Gethsemane; and He said to His disciples, 'Sit here while I pray.'" (Mark 14:32, NKJV)

"And they brought Him to the place Golgotha, which is translated, Place of a Skull." (Mark 15:22, NKJV)

"And when they had come to the place called Calvary, there they crucified Him, and the criminals, one on the right hand and the other on the left." (Luke 23:33, NKJV)

Abraham came to this place of surrender with Isaac and settled once and for all that God could trust him. This place of surrender opened up tremendous provision for his life.

Jesus came to the place of surrender called Gethsemane, Golgotha and Calvary. His choice to walk into the place of surrender resulted in humanity's salvation and freedom.

The place of surrender is the place where we give our lives to God's purposes and plans even when we don't understand them. The place of surrender is a place of deep trust in God. It is a place where you settle in your heart that God is more important than your comfort or safety. Embracing this place will actually bring freedom to our lives. More importantly, it will open ways for others to experience freedom as well.

Every time I have come to the place of surrender, I have experienced tremendous results both internally and externally. I have seen situations changed and watched God open new doors and adventures.

What will your place of surrender yield? What results will play out before you as you enter this place and establish it in your heart?

The place of prayer, the place of holiness, and the place of surrender are all places we need to establish in our lives if we are going to walk through this journey.

The Story of Jacob—Navigating Difficulties

If we are going to succeed in life, we need to be able to understand and navigate the difficult times that we all will face. Everyone will go through troubling times at some point—times whose purpose you may not clearly understand. Navigating these times *with faith* is crucial to getting to your destiny and experiencing all that God has for you.

In Genesis 32, we have the story of a God-initiated encounter. Jacob was about to face his brother Esau for the first time in a very long time.

Jacob had previously deceived Esau out of something that was rightfully his and then fled the situation to escape his brother's anger. Eventually, Jacob and Esau were on a collision course to meet and Jacob was obviously concerned.

Jacob decides to spend some alone time to gather his thoughts. In the story we find Jacob wrestling with what he thought was an angel but was actually God Himself.

We can learn several things from this story. The first is that God has places that He wants us to enter whether we want to or not. Sometimes, we find ourselves in a job situation or a relational conflict that is creating internal anxiety. Have you ever found yourself wrestling with God? Maybe you're in a situation that you can't get out. Maybe you're feeling backed into a corner and there's no way out. God could be trying to get your attention! His intention is that we encounter Him in that place.

In my early years of working, I had a boss that use to goad me almost every day. He knew I was a believer and would swear at me and try his best to get under my skin. Many times I wanted to yell back or say some choice words. Sometimes, to be honest, I failed miserably at representing Christ.

Each time I felt like I had failed, I found God challenging me to change and adjust my heart towards this man.

There may be parts of our nature or character that God wants to deal with. Like Jacob, there are moments in each of our lives when it is easier to run than wrestle or deal with the issues in our heart. However, when we say YES to God, we need to let Him speak deeply and intentionally to our hearts. Jacob was in a place where he was about to encounter God in a very personal and powerful way. It was a place that would transform his life and identity forever.

There are two key words in this passage that stand out to me. The first word is Jabbok, it is a place of pouring forth and pouring out. When we are backed into a corner, we come to a place where we need to pour out our hearts before God.

The second word is *Peniel*, which means "the face of God". Peniel is that place where we see God face to face and He begins to challenge us to deeper levels of growth and change. God wants to change your name like He changed Jacob's name. He wants to address all that you are and will become. Jacob was declared a prince with God. God always sees us differently than how others see us or we see ourselves.

Peniel is a place where we are faced with our mistakes and failures. We need to allow God to correct them and bring healing and deliverance in order for us to move forward.

Don't let the pain of your past sabotage the promise of your future.

The Story of Joseph—Waiting for Dreams

"He sent a man before them—Joseph—who was sold as a slave. They hurt his feet with fetters He was laid in irons. Until the time that his word came to pass, the word of the LORD tested him." (Psalm 105:17-19, NKJV)

In Ephesians 4:27, we are encouraged to give "no place to the devil" in our lives. The enemy wants to occupy spaces that are designed for the presence of God. When we give him a place, we risk being bound. We will be held back from experiencing all that God has for us.

The enemy would have you defeated but God is looking to establish your faith in Him and a belief that all things work together for good to those who love Him and are called according to His purpose. Joseph, as we will see understood this.

Joseph found himself in the place of testing. As a young man, he received a great vision from God and decided to share it with his brothers. Unfortunately, his brothers did not like what this meant for them. Jealousy began to plague their hearts and they set out to destroy Joseph's life.

When we decide to embrace the places to which God calls us and move forward with the vision He gives us, things begin to happen. Sometimes, it seems to be the exact opposite of what we expect. We anticipate good days but find ourselves dealing instead with rejection, trouble and hardship. We come into a place of testing. No matter what we go through God always has a plan. Nothing takes Him by surprise!

Job—A Spirit of Endurance

"For you have need of endurance, so that after you have done the will of God, you may receive the promise." *(Hebrews 10:36, NKJV)*

We need to develop a spirit of endurance in our lives. Endurance is the ability to stand under pressure or trial. Endurance is the ability to live from God's eternal view. Endurance is the ability to have a long-term perspective. God sets eternity in our hearts!

"Testing clears the mind, removes the superficial, and exposes the temporal and wrong views of life." *(Frank Damazio)*[2]

In the book of Job, there is an exchange between God and the enemy about one of God's servants. The book shows the pain and testing Job went through and eventually how God brings clarity to the whole situation.

"Testings originate in the mind and will of God to expose our weakness and deliver us from those things that hide deep within our character that could harm or even destroy us." *(Frank Damazio)*[2]

"Then the LORD said to Satan, 'Have you considered My servant Job, that there is none like him on the earth, a blameless and upright man, one who fears God and shuns evil?'" (Job 1:8, NKJV)

One of my favourite quotes from the Holy Spirit Filled Bible about the test of Job highlights for me the need for a fresh perspective in how we view life and its trials of faith:

Job is declared by God Himself to be blameless and, upright, and yet he is tried – not because of his unrighteousness but in spite of his righteousness. His trial was to establish his righteousness, as well as to give him deeper insight into his relationship with God and a greater understanding of his own nature. While the enemy's goal was to prove him a sinner, God's goal was to establish forever the sincerity of Job's faith. God does not allow trials to see if we will fail; He allows trials to strengthen our faith. The trial is in fact, a statement of God's faith in our faithfulness and integrity. (Charles E Blair - Holy Spirit Filled Bible)[3]

Sometimes, circumstances in our lives overwhelm us. They seem to bury us with no way out. We can become frustrated, discouraged and lose our joy. Being overwhelmed happens to all of us. But there is an answer.

Psalm 61:2 says, "From the end of the earth I will cry to you, when my heart is overwhelmed; lead me to the rock that is higher than I" (NKJV).

"We need to go to a higher place where God can give us peace, mercy and strength even in the midst of overwhelming circumstances. The circumstances may not change but His sufficient grace and peace will guard our hearts." (A. Coones Jr.)[4]

The Wilderness

"And you shall remember that the Lord your God led you all the way these forty years in the wilderness, to humble you and test you, to know what was in your heart, whether you would keep His commandments or not." (Deuteronomy 8:2 2, NKJV)

One of the places we will go through is what the Bible calls "the wilderness". Prior to starting His ministry, Jesus was led by the Spirit into the wilderness.

According to Matthew 4:1, "Jesus was led up by the Spirit into the wilderness to be tempted by the devil." Moses also experienced the wilderness when he ran from Egypt after killing the Egyptian worker who was beating an Israelite slave.

"God directly or indirectly guides a person into a materially or spiritually dry and desolate place, where no fruit is seen or experienced." (Frank Damazio)[5]

The wilderness is a place of hiddenness and obscurity. It's a place where we are left alone with God. God's hand is upon us, polishing our lives and character. He's getting us ready to be used for His purposes in a greater way.

"And He has made my mouth like a sharp sword; in the shadow of His hand He has hidden me, and made me a polished shaft; In His quiver He has hidden me." (Isaiah 49:2, NKJV)

Although we may feel like we are in a place of hiddenness, nothing is really hidden from God. What is darkness to us is not really darkness to the Lord at all; He sees everything. When we feel hidden and in darkness, God is still watching, working and shaping our lives for His purposes and intentions.

*"I could ask the darkness to hide me and the light around me to become night— but even in darkness I cannot hide from you. **To you the night shines as bright as day. Darkness and light are the same to you**.... My frame was not hidden from You, when I was made in secret, And skilfully wrought in the lowest parts of the earth." (Psalm 139:11-12, NKJV)*

Dark times of hiddenness require a deep trust and reliance in a great God.

*"Who among you fears the LORD? Who obeys the voice of His Servant? **Who walks in darkness and has no light**? Let him trust in the name of the LORD and rely upon his God." (Isaiah 50:10, NKHV)*

The wilderness is a place of preparation for what lies ahead in the journey. God will hide us in His quiver as an arrow ready to be shot out towards its intended target.

The wilderness is a place of challenge and the development of convictions. Moses was challenged by God to see himself differently. Called to a higher way of thinking, he was challenged to believe that God would have him do things that would take faith and courage beyond his natural ability.

In seasons of testing—wilderness experiences—we need to remain faithful. We need to continue to serve the Lord in the areas we are called to, believing that God is in that place and working things into our lives for His good.

God sees your perseverance and willingness to allow Him to work in your life. He sees your faithfulness and giving of your time, talent and treasures. He sees your sacrifice and your service when no one else sees.

Are you in a season of testing or wilderness? Take hope! God is moving and working to bring about His glory in your life. Take this time to let God work into and out of you what is necessary to go to the next level.

Ultimately, the places we establish and the places we go through are necessary for us to get to the places God has for us to experience.

The Place of Inheritance

*"By faith Abraham obeyed when he was called to go out to the place which he would receive as an **inheritance**. And he went out, not knowing where he was going." (Hebrews 11:8, NKJV)*

God has always wanted each of us to enter into a place of inheritance, a land of promise, a land where our potential is realized, satisfied and fulfilled both individually and as a local church.

The place of promise represents a place of freedom and deliverance. Psalm 18:19 says, "He brought me forth also into a large place; he delivered me, because he delighted in me." The place of promise is where blessing and fruit are flowing in our lives. Resources become readily available and enemies that we've struggled to defeat are defeated.

Judges 18:10 describes it this way: When you go, you will come to a secure people and a large land. For God has given it into your hands, **a place where there is no lack of anything** that is on the earth. (NKJV)

The inheritance that is in Christ is where faith is restored and increased. We begin to see miracles, healings, signs and wonders take place.

The place of inheritance is a wonderful place of encounter in God. Acts 4:31 says, "And when they had prayed, the place where they were assembled together was shaken; and they were all filled with the Holy Spirit, and they spoke the word of God with boldness." The enemy doesn't want believers to experience this because it signals his defeat in our lives.

GOD WANTS US TO RECEIVE OUR INHERITANCE IN CHRIST!

Heavenly Places

"Blessed be the God and Father of our Lord Jesus Christ, who hath blessed us with all spiritual blessings in heavenly places in Christ." (Ephesians 1:3, NKJV)

"...to the intent that now unto the principalities and powers in heavenly places might be known by the church the manifold wisdom of God." (Ephesians 3:10, NKJV)

*"There are many who take the phrase, 'heavenly places,' which appears several times in the book of Ephesians as a reference to heaven after we die, but if you do this, you will miss the whole import of Paul's letter. While it does talk about going to heaven someday, it is talking primarily about the life you live right now. The heavenly places are not off in some distant reach of space or on some planet or star; they are **simply the realm of invisible reality** in which the Christian lives now, in contact with God, and in the conflict with the devil in which we are all daily engaged. **It is to the invisible realm of earth**—not that which you can see, hear, taste, or feel—but that spiritual kingdom which surrounds us on all sides and which constantly influences and affects us, whether for good or evil, depending upon our wilful choice and our relationship to these invisible powers. Those are the heavenly places. In this realm, in which every one of us lives, the apostle declares that God has already **blessed us with every spiritual blessing.** That is, he has given us all that it takes to live in our present circumstances and relationships. Peter says the same thing in his second letter: His divine power has granted to us all*

things that pertain to life and godliness (2 Peter 1:3). That means that when you receive Jesus Christ as your Lord, **you have already received all that God ever intends to give you.** *The weakest believer holds in his hands all that is ever possessed by the mightiest saint of God. We already have everything, because we have Christ, and in him is every spiritual blessing and all that pertains to life and godliness.* **Thus we have what it takes to live life as God intended.** *Any failure, therefore, is not because we are lacking anything, but because we have not appropriated what is already ours." (Ray Stedman)*[6]

When we say YES to our place, we come into a time of execution of God's plans and purposes for our lives. Everything we have gone through comes into focus and we see it as being a part of something bigger than ourselves.

Joseph came to that realization as he faced his brothers. In Genesis 50:19-20, he says to them, "Do not fear, for am I in the place of God? As for you, you meant evil against me, but God meant it for good, to bring it about that many people should be kept alive, as they are today."

Although it had taken many years of testing, trials, and wilderness moments before his dream came to pass, Joseph understood that he was in the place of God and that all of the struggles, tests and delays were really a preparation for where God had taken him. He had maintained a right heart. He had maintained a right attitude. He had maintained a right spirit. And he was able to see that God was in everything and that He was in control.

I hope as you read and reflect on this chapter that you will look deeply at your life with a new perspective on the struggles you're currently going through. Galatians 6:9 says, "Don't grow weary in well doing for in due season you will reap your reward."

God is working in your life and will bring a full manifestation of His work in due season.

Will you take time to thank God and let Him do what He needs to do in your life? Will you take time to search your heart to see what needs to be looked at? Will you take time to believe God for great days ahead? God is working in your heart and life to accomplish His will and purpose.

Say YES to the House of God

*"Meanwhile, Jacob left Beersheba and traveled toward Haran. At sundown he arrived at **a good place** to set up camp and stopped there for the night. Jacob found a stone to rest his head against and lay down to sleep. As he slept, he dreamed of a stairway that reached from the earth up to heaven. And he saw the angels of God going up and down the stairway. At the top of the stairway stood the Lord, and he said, "**I am the Lord**, the God of your grandfather Abraham, and the God of your father, Isaac. The ground you are lying on belongs to you. **I am giving it to you and your descendants. Your descendants will be as numerous as the dust of the earth!** They will spread out in all directions—to the west and the east, to the north and the south. And all the families of the earth will be blessed through you and your descendants. What's more, I am with you, and I will protect you wherever you go. One day I will bring you back to this land. I will not leave you until I have finished giving you everything I have promised you." Then Jacob awoke from his sleep and said, **"Surely the Lord is in this place**, and **I wasn't even aware of it!"** [1]But he was also afraid and said, "What an awesome place this is! **It is none other than the house of God**, **the very gateway to heaven**!" The next morning Jacob got up very early. He took the stone he had rested his head against, and he set it*

*upright as a memorial pillar. Then he poured olive oil over it. He named that place Bethel (which means "house of God"), although it was previously called Luz. Then Jacob made this vow: "If God will indeed be with me and protect me on this journey, and if he will provide me with food and clothing, and if I return safely to my father's home, then the Lord will certainly be my God. **And this memorial pillar I have set up will become a place for worshiping God, and I will present to God a tenth of everything he gives me."** (Genesis 28:10-22, NLT)*

The Church has taken a beating lately. Many people want to leave their local churches and instead watch services on the internet or create their own house meetings. I believe in the CHURCH! I believe it is the house of God where His presence comes and ministers to His people. The house of God is a place where lives can be changed and set on course for great destiny.

The house of God is a good place. It's a place to set up camp and stay awhile. The house of God is actually a portal into heaven's activity. Jacob's dream gives us clues as to what is happening in heaven. While dreaming he saw angels going up and down the ladder. The Scripture makes it clear angels do exist, that they are the Lord's servants sent to minister to His church (Hebrews 1:7) and that they have been released to protect the saints of God (Psalms 91:11).

Jesus confirms that He is the ladder that Jacob dreamed about, that angelic activity would come through Him and that our belief in Jesus gives us access into heaven. Jesus is the foundation upon which the house of God is built.

"Do not forget to entertain strangers, for by so doing some have unwittingly entertained angels." (Hebrews 13:2, NKJ

While I was in Ghana this past summer, there was a serious flood that took the lives of about 200 people. It was a really sad day in the life of the people of Ghana. During the flooding, a group of people tried to stay safe at a gas station. Unfortunately, the gas station exploded and took about 90 lives.

While at church the following Sunday, I heard the pastor share a story of a lady who was at the station and heard a voice tell her to run. As she began to run, the station exploded. She continued to hear the voice speaking, telling her to run through the fire.

The lady kept running. An old man came alongside her, took her hand and said, "Follow me." They ran together through the fire and the flood. She got to the other side and ran up a flight of stairs. As she looked back, she saw the devastation caused by the fire and flood. She then turned to thank the man but he was gone.

Isaiah 42:3 came to her mind: "When you pass through the waters, I will be with you; And through the rivers, they shall not overflow you. When you walk through the fire, you shall not be burned, nor shall the flame scorch you" (NKJV). This was a divine moment in which angelic activity took place in this woman's life.

When we come into the house of God, we open ourselves to heaven's activity and God begins to move on our behalf.

Jacob heard the voice of God speaking to him at the top of the ladder and, when he awoke, he understood that he was in an awesome place—the very house of God.

All throughout Scripture, when the heavens were opened, God revealed Himself in mighty ways. Ezekiel says, "The heavens were opened and I saw visions of God" (Ezekiel 1:1, NKJV). Ezekiel saw God in all His glory and majesty.

God wants to reveal Himself to each of us in unique ways. He wants to show us who He is, displaying His goodness and greatness. He is a God who loves us. He is a wonderful healer and deliverer. He is a God who is not afraid to show Himself to His people.

"When He had been baptized, Jesus came up immediately from the water; and behold, the heavens were opened to Him, and He saw the Spirit of God descending like a dove and coming upon Him. And suddenly a voice came from heaven, saying, 'This is My beloved Son, in whom I am well pleased.'" (Matthew 3:16-17, NKJV)

As Jesus was coming out of the waters of baptism, the heavens opened and God began to speak to His Son and the people around Him. God began to affirm His Son, to tell Him that He was well pleased.

God wants to do the same for each and every one of us. He wants us to know He is well pleased with our lives.

The heavens opened for John and he saw Jesus riding on a white horse revealing Him to be the conquering King of kings:

Now I saw heaven opened, and behold, a white horse and He who sat on him was called Faithful and True, and in righteousness He judges and makes war. (Revelation 19:11, NKJV)

God wants to show us who He is and that He is faithful and true, making war and our enemies and defeating our foes.

When Jacob looked up into heaven, a number of things began to take place: At the top of the stairway stood the Lord, and He said, "I am the Lord, the God of your grandfather Abraham, and the God of your father, Isaac. **The ground you are lying on belongs to you. I am giving it to you and your descendants. Your descendants will be as numerous as the dust of the earth! They will spread out in all directions**—to the west and the east, to the north and the south. And all the **families of the earth**

will be blessed through you and your descendants." (Genesis 28:13-14, NKJV)

Jacob heard God announce that He was a generational God, that He loved Jacob's father and grandfather, and that He would also love Jacob. God was interested in generations and He is still interested in generations today.

God has always had a group of people from every generation who He called out to Himself.

There have always been people of faith from every generation who have embraced God, leaned upon His ways and developed relationship with Him.

God reminded Jacob of the promises made long ago to his father and grandfather. He promised that they would one day be a numerous people that would bless the other people of the earth. Jacob was lying on the very ground that God had promised to His family.

When we come into relationship with God and into the house of God, He begins to declare His purposes, promises and intentions for our lives just as He did with Jacob. God has many thoughts that He thinks toward us and His thoughts are good and not of evil but to actually give us a future and a hope. *(Jeremiah 29:11)*

It's exciting to be in a place where God speaks, to be where He announces to us that He wants to prosper and bless us and that he wants to make us fruitful.

There are places that God wants us to occupy, these are places where, in the past, we would not have been able to go, places we had no right to enter because we were held back, but God makes a way when we can't see a way. He helps us live and walk in victory. Eventually, as we continue to walk in His ways, we begin to be a blessing to those around us. Our lives are touched by the divine presence and that impact on our lives can make a difference in the people we know.

While on a trip to Cambodia, I visited the Russian market. Pastor Jason Prosser, who I was with, took me around to specific booths of people he knew from his church community so we could support them. As we were leaving, a lady came up to Pastor Jason. He knew her, so we walked to her booth as well.

This lady had had a rough life. Her abusive husband had poured acid on her and she was badly deformed as a result. She told us that, for 16 years, she had walked around the market selling her goods to make a living, within that time, she had come to know Jesus.

Since then, she found peace and joy, and it was evident on her countenance and since being connected to the house of God, Jesus had touched and transformed this woman's heart. He had declared His intentions to bless and prosper her. Her life, although still difficult and painful, was now prospering. She now had a booth to sell her goods in one place. She was grateful to the Lord for His help in prospering her, and looking after her and her daughter. She was growing in her love for God and His house.

It was so moving to see how God turns adversity into victory! She was happy to give me a discount on her goods and present me with a beautiful picture. I was more than willing to bless her beyond her expectations because her life was a living testimony of what can happen when a life surrenders to Jesus and gets established in the house of God.

In his encounter with God, Jacob heard God begin to affirm that He was a relational God who wanted to connect with Him and assist him in his life. *"What's more, **I am with you**, and **I will protect you** wherever you go. One day **I will bring you back** to this land. **I will not leave you** until I*

have finished giving you everything I have promised you."
(Genesis 25:15, NKJV)

"Jacob, I am with YOU!"

What an amazing statement. It really should not surprise us. God has always intentionally reached out and spent time with His people. He is intentionally present! He is Immanuel, God with us.

There are moments throughout the week when life can beat you and drag you down. You might feel like you are on your own and the weight of the journey and tests of life make you wonder where God is. Without hesitation, when I have ventured into the house of God or spent time with Him, His voice rings out crystal clear, "Insert your name" I am with you!"

"Jacob, I will protect YOU!"

We're living in very troubling times. At the time of this writing, Lebanon and Paris have been attacked; terrorists are seeking to spread fear and dread upon the earth. A number of close friends and family are struggling with serious health issues and the economies of the world are shaking. I believe it's so important for us to hear what God said to Jacob. He was on the run from his brother who he had deceived out of his birthright and was going to a foreign land. He needed to hear that God would protect him. Do you believe God is your protector?

A number of years ago, I was waiting on the Lord and had a vision. In that vision, a family member was yelling at me. I can't remember what they were upset about but I could feel the emotion of fear begin to rise up in my heart. Immediately, I looked around and thought "Where's my dad?" I couldn't find or see him. Why wasn't he there to protect me?

As I began to ponder this vision I knew there was something deeper that God was trying to show me. I heard a still small voice say to me, "You don't believe I will protect you!" In a moment, my heart was laid open before God and I realized that I didn't believe God would protect me and keep me from harm's way.

It's amazing how we try to protect and guard ourselves from being hurt, how we put up walls around us to keep things out. I had gone through a number of relational situations that had subtly begun to close my heart and cause me to want to protect myself rather than be hurt again. The Lord began to encourage me that living in relationships require risk and faith.

Since that day, I have developed many great relationships, experienced God's peace and protection many times and, whenever fear begins to grip my heart, I hear His voice saying, "I will protect you."

"Your heart has the potential to harden or soften, depending on your attitudes, decisions, and responses to life's issues!" (Brian Houston)[1]

As believers, we need to put on the shoes of the gospel of peace. We need to stand in peace.

We need to take heart at these words spoken by Jesus 2000 years ago as they ring true today: "These things I have spoken to you, that in Me you may have peace. In the world you will have tribulation; but be of good cheer, I have overcome the world" (John 16:33, NKJV).

"Jacob, I will bring you back!"

"The enemy comes to steal, kill and destroy but Jesus comes to give life and life more abundant." (John 10:10, NLT)

God is a God of restoration. He is not unaware of our situations or needs. Each of us has a story of something that was taken from our lives or something that went missing at the hands of the enemy. God will bring you back! God will restore! God will make a way to recover all that was lost.

In 2 Kings 4, we have a story of the Shummanite woman who looked after Elisha and saw tremendous miracles as a result. She had not only fed this man of God, but had even made a room for him to stay in while he was in town. Eventually, there was a famine in the land that lasted seven years. The man of God instructed her to leave everything she had worked hard to acquire with no guarantee of getting anything back.

In 2 Kings 8, Elisha's servant was speaking to the king about the miracles that had been performed by Elisha, one of which happened to be the raising of this woman's son. At that moment, the woman came to the king to request her land back. Elisha's servant saw the woman and began to talk to the king.

The king looked into the woman's situation and declared, "Restore all that was hers, and all the proceeds of the field from the day that she left the land until now" (2 Kings 8:6, NKJV).

I have found as we stay in the house of God, He will restore to our lives all that has been lost or stolen. Zechariah 9:12 states, "Return to the stronghold, you prisoners of hope. Even today I declare that I will restore double to you." (NKJV).

Restoration

In 1996, my wife and I decided to move our young family to a new church. It was a great move spiritually; we had gone through a serious church issue and needed a place of refuge and the new church had invited me to come on staff as well.

However, two significant things took place with this move. First, we had to sell our house. Due to the housing market at the time and the fact that we had put money into renovating our home, if we sold we would lose about $45,000. Secondly, in order to come on staff, I would have to take a pay cut of approximately $25,000-$30,000 a year.

Many would look at this and say, "Did you really hear from God?" We knew, however, that this was the Lord so we moved ahead, believing that God would watch over us. Those early years were a struggle and yet we had a peace that God would restore to us as we were faithful to honour Him.

A number of years later, we decided to sell the house we were living in. By this time, my income had doubled and we were able to sell our house for almost double what we paid for it. God will restore double!

We need to stay in the stronghold of hope! Hope is an expectation of good things to come. Do you have hope in your heart, an expectation of good things to come? Don't let the enemy steal your hope! Believe that good things are coming your way!

"Jacob, I will not leave you until I have finished giving you everything I have promised you." (Genesis 28:15, NKJV)

WOW! What a promise from God! We already have spoken about saying YES to the promises of God but this is an amazing affirmation to Jacob. It reminds me of the promise from Jesus in John 14:18: "No, I will not abandon you or leave you as orphans in the storm—I will come to you" (NKJV). Philippians 1:6 says, "He who began a good work in you will be faithful to complete it" (NKJV).

When we say YES to the house of God, we begin to hear God affirm His commitment to us. I have countless stories of being in the house of God and hearing again and again His voice affirming His promises to my life.

When you stay committed to God and His house, you begin to see many great things take place in your life and in the lives of others. In the house of God, I've watched God grow a church significantly; I've seen many people come to know the Lord; and I've watched my son grow, develop his gifts and calling and meet and marry his wife.

My wife and I also developed many lifelong relationships with people we've met in the house of God.

When we say YES to the house of God, worship is established in our hearts as a sacred place:

Then Jacob awoke from his sleep and said, **"Surely the Lord is in this place**, and **I wasn't even aware of it!"** But he was also afraid and said, "What an awesome place this is! **It is none other than the house of God, the very gateway to heaven!"** The next morning Jacob got up very early. He took the stone he had rested his head against, and he set it upright as a memorial pillar.

Then he poured olive oil over it. He named that place Bethel (which means "house of God"), although it was previously called Luz. Then Jacob made this vow: "If God will indeed be with me and protect me on this journey, and if he will provide me with food and clothing, and if I return safely to my father's home, then the Lord will certainly be my God. And this memorial pillar I have set up will become a place for worshiping God, and I will present to God a tenth of everything He gives me" (Genesis 28:16-22**).**

Have you ever had a situation take place and, afterward, realized that God was in it but you were oblivious? Jacob awoke and came to that realization. He realized that God was in that place. He was in awe that God would meet him and speak to him!

Whenever we encounter God, we experience certain emotions and develop certain convictions. These are significant moments that we need to capture.

Joy is a wonderful expression when you encounter God deeply. Every time we step into the house of God or place of encounter, He begins to touch our hearts deeply and fills our lives with joy. A sense of awe wells up in our hearts that the Creator of the universe would stoop and look into our lives with such care and concern.

We need to honour these moments. They become memorial stones in our journey. They become part of the testimony of God's work in our lives and a weapon to defeat discouragement and unbelief.

When we encounter God, we need to determine to serve and love Him in greater ways than we are currently. Every encounter with God is an opportunity to grow and be strengthened in both our values and our purpose.

When we encounter God, we also begin to worship more freely and deliberately. Our hearts begin to align with who we are to become. Jesus begins to take center place in our lives.

We begin to be generous with our time, talents and treasure. Generosity becomes a core value in our lives. Jacob decided to give a tenth of all that he had. In modern days we call that a tithe—10% of your income.

Living by this principle is a choice that comes out of an encounter moment.

Over the years, my family has given more than 10% each year to the house of God, as well as served countless hours giving our time and gifts to build God's house.

Tithing is just the beginning for a generous person. Generosity involves more than just money; it involves the giving of your life to something greater than your comfort.

Please don't miss this: An encounter with God will produce significant change in you that will result in a noticeable difference to those around you! God wants to show up and touch our lives, to bring healing and change to the very core beliefs we have.

"Let us hold fast the confession of our hope without wavering, for He who promised is faithful. And let us consider one another in order to stir up love and good works, not forsaking the assembling of ourselves together, as is the manner of some, but exhorting one another, and so much the more as you see the Day approaching." *(Hebrews 10:23-25, NKJV)*

God wants us to live our lives in community, in connection with other likeminded believers who possess an unquenchable hope and unwavering confession. He wants us to live in connection with a group of people who believe in a faithful God who wants to speak and relate to us in supernatural ways. He wants us to consider each other, stirring each other in love and good works. We need to recognize that the time we live in requires us to value meeting together even more than in previous times. God wants to encounter us and show us who He is and who we can become.

Will you say YES to the house of God? Don't allow the spirit of the age to draw you into isolating yourself from God's people and His house.

Say YES to Reaching One Person at a Time

Jesus was on a mission. He was seeking to reach lost and hurting people, to impact their lives one person at a time. He was willing to divert His plans to go and see someone in need.

In Mark 5, there is an amazing story of a man who, for many years, had one bad day after another. He was literally plagued with demons and couldn't break free. His life had taken a definite turn for the worst and he couldn't get out of this daily battle. Many had tried to help this man but were unable to do anything that would bring relief. Yet, as soon as Jesus stepped into the scene, the man ran and worshipped Him: "When he saw Jesus from afar, he ran and worshiped Him" (Mark 5:6, NKJV).

Jesus quickly put a stop to this man's pain and brought freedom and instant relief to him.

"Then they came to Jesus, and saw the one who had been demon-possessed and had the legion, sitting and clothed and in his right mind." (Mark 5:15, NKJV)

This man was immediately transformed by one interaction with Jesus. He wanted to repay Jesus by following Him for the rest of his life. But Jesus did not permit the man to go with Him. Instead, He encouraged him to go and tell his friends the great things God had done:

However, Jesus did not permit him, but said to him, "Go home to your friends, and tell them what great things the Lord has done for you, and how He has had compassion on you." And he departed and began to proclaim in Decapolis all that Jesus had done for him; and all marvelled. (Mark 5:19-20, NKJV)

When our lives have been impacted by a touch from Jesus, all He asks is that we declare His goodness to others, that we are witnesses of His love and power in our lives.

Penn Jillette, the atheist illusionist and comedian, said the following:

I don't respect people who don't proselytize. I don't respect that at all. If you believe that there's a heaven and hell and people could be going to hell or not getting eternal life or whatever, and you think that it's not really worth telling them this because it would make it socially awkward. .... How much do you have to hate somebody to believe that everlasting life is possible and not tell them that?[1]

This cuts to the heart of who we need to be and what our lives need to be about.

Everyone has a circle of influence that they impact on a daily basis!

Our task is to permeate that circle with the love and goodness of Jesus Christ. When we neglect this task, we miss out on experiencing the divine connections God has for us and seeing the freedom that can come to people's lives. Acts 10:38 says, "And you know that God anointed Jesus of Nazareth with the Holy Spirit and with power. Then Jesus went around doing good and healing all who were oppressed by the devil, for God was with him."

Every believer and follower of Christ has been provided with two primary means to win the world for Jesus. First and foremost, we have the message of the gospel of Jesus Christ. This gospel is something that we don't need to be ashamed of.

In Romans 1:16-17, Paul says, "For I am not ashamed of the gospel of Christ, for it is the power of God to salvation for everyone who believes, for the Jew first and also for the Greek. For in it the righteousness of God is revealed." The gospel is the good news that Jesus came to earth to redeem man from his sin-stained life. It is the promise that freedom and abundant life is possible for everyone who believes that Jesus is the Son of God.

The second method that believers can use to win the world for Jesus is to manifest the life of Jesus in their lives on a daily basis. 1 Peter 3:1-2 says, "In the same way ... even if some refuse to obey the Good News, your godly lives will speak to them without any words. They will be won over by observing your pure and reverent lives." One of the greatest hindrances to the gospel is the life of a follower of Jesus Christ. We've all been impacted by people who claim to know Christ yet misrepresent who He really is. The challenge is to live out the gospel in our lives before preaching it to others.

Once, while Christmas shopping in Toronto, a man came up to my family and I outside of a store and screamed,

"You're either choosing to go hell or choosing to go to heaven." I just smiled and walked away. He probably meant well, but his message was not good news and his behaviour did not represent the Jesus of the Bible. For me, the model of the New Testament is one of grace and kindness, showing people a good God who wants to connect with them—a God who loves them deeply enough to send His Son to die in their place.

A recent survey by The Institute for American Church Growth asked over 10,000 people this question: "What was responsible for your coming to Christ?"

Their replies:

> a. I had a special need - 2%
> b. I just walked in - 3%
> c. I like the minister - 6%
> d. I visited there - 1%
> e. I like the Bible classes - 5%
> f. I attended a gospel meeting - 0.5%
> g. I liked the programs - 3%
> h. **A friend or relative invited me - 79%**[2]

Does this not tell us something? Effectively sharing our faith is not so much a matter of mechanics but of a genuine, honest and overflowing relationship with Jesus Christ.

"People will forget what you said, people will forget what you did, but people will never forget how you made them feel." Maya Angelou

There are many key issues facing people today. There are seven billion people on the earth today but many are lonelier than ever. People can be in a crowd yet lost in their own lonely world. Although we live in an information age with everything at our disposal, many feel disconnected from family and friends.

The fear of death and the unknown is terrorizing people every day as they seek to find inner peace. As things rapidly advance in the world and we hear negative news day after day, the feeling of being out of control is real. Chaos seems to abound and it doesn't seem like things are getting any better.

Very few people live with purpose in their lives. They seem to exist during the week so they can leave it all behind for a weekend of pleasure and fantasy. Unfortunately, it's back to the grind on Monday! Many drown their sorrows in illicit relationships, drugs and alcohol.

Many people carry an inner emptiness, despair and a sense of feeling lost. The things our society offers to cure all ails have under-delivered and caused a deep angst in people's lives. Consumer debt has escalated due to the "eye never being satisfied". People want the latest and greatest advancement in technology, the latest car or a bigger home. Selfishness has gripped people's hearts more than ever and they are living for the present rather than for eternity.

"Now may the God of hope fill you with all joy and peace in believing, that you may abound in hope by the power of the Holy Spirit." (Romans 15:13, NKJV)

Now more than at any time, the world is in need of a Saviour, a God of hope! The world is in need of people who are living in peace and joy abounding in the power of the Holy Spirt. The message of the Bible is that "the thief has come to steal, kill and destroy but Jesus has come to give us life and life more abundantly" (John 10:10). The Church has a tremendous opportunity to reach a society in trouble and offer it hope and peace. Jesus is the answer!

In Luke 15, Jesus was hanging out with the tax collectors and sinners when the religious folk began to complain about His selection of acquaintances.

In their world, these people were beneath them and didn't deserve the time of day. According to Luke 19:10, however, Jesus came "to seek and save those who are lost". He loved these people and wanted to reach them.

EVERYONE IS LOST AT SOME POINT AND IN NEED OF A SAVIOUR.

In Luke 15, Jesus unpacks three separate stories to teach the religious leaders of that day about God's heart towards the lost. In these stories we have three lost situations: a lost sheep, a lost coin and two lost sons.

All of these objects represented something of value and importance. Jesus wanted us to see the obvious—that HE considers the lost valuable, important and of great worth.

In our first story, we have a lost sheep who had wandered from the flock. Many shepherds at that time were community shepherds who looked after the whole community's sheep. It was a big deal to lose even one sheep.

The whole community would have felt this loss and would have suffered. Losing this one sheep required a drastic search.

In our second story, we have a coin that was lost. The woman's coin was precious to her for more than its monetary value. Every woman would collect 10 coins and fashion them as part of their wedding headdress. These coins also served as part of their dowry. Losing this one coin required a drastic search.

The story of the lost or prodigal son is really about *two* sons. The first son is a spectacular sinner. His decisions led him to depths of profound loss and isolation. This son found himself in places that no one in their right mind would ever want to be. The second son is a self-righteous, law-abiding person, much like Jesus' critics.

This son was lost in a performance mentality and needed saving from himself. Jesus may well have told this story primarily as a challenge to similar people. Each son was lost in his own unique way. Each required drastic measures to reach him.

GOD SENT JESUS TO RECAPTURE OUR ATTENTION FROM THINGS THAT HAVE STOLEN OUR PROPER FOCUS.

In each of these stories, we see the passion and willingness of people to search and find what was lost. The woman was willing to clean her whole house, lighting a lamp and sweeping away the dust and dirt to find the coin. The shepherd was willing to leave the rest of the sheep and, once he found his little lost sheep, place it on his shoulders to carry it back to safety. The father of the two boys shows amazing willingness and compassion in the face of a culture that wouldn't care for the way the first son disregarded and disrespected him.

In the culture of the day, the son would have been banished from the city forever. The father's response to the second son is another amazing show of grace and compassion that would go against the culture of that day.

GOD IS PASSSIONATELY IN LOVE WITH YOU!
HE IS ALWAYS GENTLY DRAWING YOU TO HIMSELF.

"I drew them with gentle cords, with bands of love, and I was to them as those who take the yoke from their neck. I stooped and fed them." (Hosea 11:4, NKJV)

Have you ever lost something very important and then found it after a long extended search? You want to tell everyone and rejoice with those close to you. All the people in our stories responded by telling others. Friends were called, parties were thrown and joy and celebration became the experience of the day.

The stories tell of God's readiness to welcome the lost. He rejoices when they are found, even when they have no merits to plead.

The story of the two sons is a story without an ending. Although the younger son has been received into the house, the older son stands outside complaining. It is not clear whether he accepts or rejects his father's invitation to step inside. But it is clear that the father extends the same love and mercy to both his sons.

GOD ALWAYS REJOICES WHEN YOU COME TO HIM.

"The strength of the church is not in its programs, worship or building but in a people who are passionate for the Lord and the lost. A people who will open their lives to new people and go after those who are lost but don't know it."
Author Unknown

The heart of Jesus was always to look for opportunities to touch the lives of people. All throughout the New Testament, we see Him impacting the individual lives of people.

The Woman at the Well

In John chapter 4, there is another story of Jesus seeking to save the lost.

Therefore, when the Lord knew that the Pharisees had heard that Jesus made and baptized more disciples than John (though Jesus Himself did not baptize, but His disciples), He left Judea and departed again to Galilee. But He needed to go through Samaria. So He came to a city of Samaria which is called Sychar, near the plot of ground that Jacob gave to his son Joseph. Now Jacob's well was there. Jesus therefore, being wearied from His journey, sat thus by the well. It was about the sixth hour. A woman of Samaria came to draw water. Jesus said to her, "Give Me a drink." For His disciples had gone away into the city to buy food. Then the woman of Samaria said to Him, "How is it that You, being a Jew, ask a drink from me, a Samaritan woman?" For Jews have no dealings with Samaritans. Jesus answered and said to her, "If you knew the gift of God, and who it is who says to you, 'Give Me a drink,' you would have asked Him, and He would have given you living water." The woman said to Him, "Sir, You have nothing to draw with, and the well is deep. Where then do You get that living water? Are You greater than our father Jacob, who gave us the well, and drank from it himself, as well as his sons and his livestock?" Jesus answered and said to her, "Whoever drinks of this water will thirst again, but whoever drinks of the water that I shall give him will never thirst. But the water that I shall give him will become in him a fountain of water springing up into everlasting life." The woman said to Him, "Sir, give me this water, that I may not thirst, nor come here to draw." Jesus said to her, "Go, call your husband, and come here." The woman answered and said, "I have no husband." Jesus said to her, "You have well said, 'I have no husband,' for you have had five husbands, and the one whom you now have is not your husband; in that you spoke truly." The woman said to Him, "Sir, I perceive that You are a prophet. Our fathers worshiped on this mountain, and you Jews say that in Jerusalem is the place where one ought to worship." Jesus said to her, "Woman, believe Me, the hour is coming when you will neither on this mountain, nor in Jerusalem, worship the Father. You worship what you do not know; we know what we worship, for salvation is of the Jews. But the hour *is coming, and now is, when the true worshipers will worship the Father in spirit and truth; for the Father is seeking such to worship Him. God is Spirit, and those who worship Him must worship in spirit and truth." The woman said to Him, "I know that Messiah is coming" (who is called Christ). "When He comes, He will tell us all things." Jesus said to her, "I who speak to you am He." And at this point His disciples came, and they marvelled that He talked with a woman; yet no one said, "What do You seek?" or, "Why are You talking with her?" The woman then left her water pot, went her way into the city, and said to the men, "Come, see a Man who told me all things that I ever did. Could this be the Christ?" Then they went out of the city and came to Him. In the meantime His disciples urged Him, saying, "Rabbi, eat." But He said to them, "I have food to eat of which you do not know." Therefore the disciples said to one another, "Has anyone brought Him anything to eat?" Jesus said to them, "My food is to do the will of Him who sent Me, and to finish His work. Do you not say, 'There are still four months and then comes the harvest'? Behold, I say to you, lift up your eyes and look at the fields, for they are already white for harvest! And he who reaps receives wages, and gathers fruit for eternal life, that both he who sows and he who reaps may rejoice together. For in this the saying is true: 'One sows and another reaps.' I sent you to reap that for which you have not laboured; others have laboured, and you have entered into their labours." (NKJV)*

The Samaritans were Assyrians and Jews who had become mixed when the Assyrian occupation had finished.

These were the rejected and despised of the land. It was unthinkable that a Rabbi or Teacher of the Law would speak to a Samaritan, let alone a man to a woman. Jesus' mission was to break through barriers and remove obstacles to reach people. He knew this one thing about humanity: we all have issues!

John 4:4 states, "He needed to go through Samaria." Jesus was compelled by *a need*! Everyone has a deep need that they cannot be satisfied by the things life has to offer.

Jesus decided to take a step of faith and connect to a person who had a need.

Jesus used the Samaritan woman's natural need to highlight a spiritual lack in her life. Jesus wants to take our natural, add His SUPER to it and make it SUPERNATURAL! Many times, He will use the natural things that happen in our lives to bring us to our knees. He desires we acknowledge Him. In this story, Jesus used the Samaritan woman's need for water as an opening to minister to her deepest needs. He encouraged her to place her trust and satisfaction in Himself—the Living Water. He was the one who could truly satisfy.

Jesus models for us what it's like to respond to a need and help someone deal with real problems and inner struggles. Jesus used a word of knowledge to speak to the issues in the Samaritan woman's character. The woman's sin had produced shame, guilt, hurt and fear, but Jesus brought her to the place of her deepest need and pain, to the sin that dried her weary soul.

"If you're going to move to your promise you need to go through your greatest relational pain." (Chris Hodges)[4]

Notice that the woman was alone at the well she was likely shunned by the other women probably because of her choices and lifestyle. The hurting rejected woman needed to let go of her past to focus on her future.

Jesus offered the woman at the well something that all her pursuits could not provide. He helped her to become a true disciple. Jesus taught her about God-centered worship.

He drew her into understanding what true worship was all about—the process of daily surrendering to Gods will and His ways.

This divine encounter with Jesus touched the woman so deeply that she wanted to tell her friends about the impact of this man on her life. So she *ran* to tell them about her newfound belief in the Messiah. Whenever a person is impacted by the message of the gospel, he or she wants to declare to everyone the great things the Lord has done!

A wonderful picture ensued as Jesus was discussing His encounter with this woman with His disciples. He began to tell them that the harvest was ready—not in a few months, but right now. He said, "Lift up your eyes for the fields are white for harvest." And as they looked towards the town, people were coming through the fields with the woman leading them. The whole town had come to see what great things this man had done for the woman.

They wanted to experience it for themselves. There is always a spiritual harvest ready to be gathered. We must make ourselves available to reach people!

I want to close this chapter with a story that happened at Universal Studios a few years back. My family and I were walking through the park along with hundreds of others. All of a sudden, I heard a scream and a woman began to yell, "Michael! Michael!"

I ran up to the woman and asked what was wrong. With panic in her voice, she told me that her little boy with Down's syndrome had somehow gotten off his cord and was lost. This was a pretty big family, so all the kids started to run around screaming his name.

The father took off running toward the front gate. Can you imagine how this family felt? Their little boy was lost in a big park with hundreds of people milling around.

My family began to search as well. I went into stores and looked under clothes racks and in washrooms. We looked for workers and recruited their help. After about 15 minutes, as I came out of a store, I saw a worker come out of a ride with a young boy.

"Are you Michael?" I asked.

"Yes," he replied, unconcerned that he was lost.

All of a sudden, I heard the mom scream, "Michael!" She ran to him, dropped to her knees and, through tears, began to passionately tell him, "Michael, I love you! Oh Michael, I love you!"

Then the brothers and sisters came running over and, also with tears, said, "We love you, Michael!" Michael was oblivious to what was going on but the family was visibly moved.

It was a very emotional moment and I, too, had tears in my eyes. I asked the brother to call their father and let him know that Michael was found.

Then I asked the mom if she was okay. She said yes and, after a few minutes, my family and I went on our way.

As I pondered this experience, a number of things came to mind. First of all, the reaction of the people in the park was basically nonexistent. They were going about their routine without any consideration for the lost little boy. They were apathetic to the plight of his heartbroken mother.

The family, on the other hand, was in panic mode. As they searched the area, they didn't care how loudly they yelled Michael's name. They were concerned about one thing and one thing only: finding their little boy.

Our family was deeply moved by their situation. We were willing to give up our time and energy to search for the little boy and, once he was found, we were overjoyed that he was reunited with his family.

When Michael came out of the ride exit, his family reacted with love and gratefulness that Michael was found! The mother didn't yell or get angry because Michael had gone missing. Instead, tears of joy and happiness streamed down her face.

What is God's reaction when the lost go missing? Is He angry or upset? I think His reaction is like the mother's. He is happy and full of joy that the lost have been found.

When you and I are faced with lost people, what will our reaction be? Will we be more concerned with our own needs? Or will we engage ourselves in the task of looking for them? What will our response be when the lost are found? Will we be angry or rejoice and be happy?

When we say YES to reaching one person at a time each day, we get to look for people who are in need of Jesus. We get to use our gifts and talents to impact people's lives with the goodness of God.

The most important thing you and I can do with our lives is to meet people where they are at and let them know how important they are, that God has a plan for them and that He loves them deeply.

The gospel is pretty simple. We just have to be obedient to reach out to those who are in our path. We need to recognize the needs they have and show them that God can supernaturally meet those needs with His love and power.

Will You Say YES?

We've come to the end our time together and, as we've seen, there are many things to which we need to say YES. Each of the areas discussed is important in developing our walk with Christ.

We must be willing to live deeply in Him allowing His Spirit to touch every part of our lives.

Before we can say YES to all that God has for us, we must be willing to say NO to the things that would hold us back from our destiny. Have you decided to leave some things behind? Have you decided to say NO to the things that would hold you back? Remember before you can truly say YES you need to say NO.

Saying YES to who you are in Christ is a crucial step and will be the launching pad for you to say YES to His great promises in your life and to say YES to a prosperous soul.

Who you are in Christ will not only give you access to His promises, it will also cause you to be abundant in all areas of living. Jesus came to give us life and life more abundantly. Each of us need to live large with a resounding YES in our spirit.

Once we have these things in place and our soul is at rest, we can then prepare ourselves to say YES to being shaken and fighting the good fight of faith. When things begin to happen in our lives, when we feel the shaking of God or the engagement of the enemy we need to already be saying YES to God working in our lives. He wants to do a great work in and through us. Saying YES will cause us to walk in victory and fulfill His will for our lives.

Every believer will need to find their place in God to live at their best. When we find our place in God we begin to walk into our destiny and purpose set out by Him. God wants us to find our place so we can enjoy using our gifts and abilities in His house. God wants to reveal Himself in many ways to our lives; He regularly does this through our place in the house of God. God desires that we encounter Him and live from His presence each and every day.

When we find our place and are established in the house of God, we gain a new perspective on our purpose. We receive the affirmation and begin to operate in the calling and gifts we were designed for. We are called to reach the lost, one person at a time. There is no greater joy than to see fruit remain that you had a hand in reaching.

In Cambodia, I was privileged to meet three men who our home church has supported in ministry for approximately 15 years. They were some of the first converts in this Buddhist nation under New Life Fellowship Cambodia. They have thrived spiritually, grown in their walk with God and are some of the greatest church planters in this movement. Their local church has planted 180 churches with a vision for 500 more by 2020. They have developed a great local church, all because they said YES to Jesus and His great work in their life.

Today will you say YES to God working in your heart and mind? Will you say YES to God building your life around these principles? God wants each and every one to advance, grow and move forward.

He will do what He needs to do to bring us into His pleasure, will and destiny.

Say YES to your Identity
Say YES to the Promises of God
Say YES to a Prosperous Soul
Say YES to Being Shaken
Say YES to the Good Fight
Say YES to Your Place
Say YES to the House of God
Say YES to Reaching One Person at a Time

Footnotes

Chapter 1—Before You Say YES—Say NO!

1. Dennis Lacheney, MFI Session notes, 2014. Used by permission.
2. Joel Osteen, Twitter feed, @JoelOsteen, ca[2015].

Chapter 2—Say YES to Your Identity in Christ

1. E. Glenn Wagner, *Fire in Your bones: Ignite Your Life with Power* (Charlotte: LifeBridge Books, 2009).
2. "Identity". Dictionary.com. *Dictionary.com Unabridged*. Random House, Inc.

Chapter 3—Say YES to the Promises of God

1. A.W. Pink – "The Attributes of God -The Immutability of God", http://www.pbministries.org.
2. Charles Spurgeon, "The Treasury of David: Psalm 111", http://www.romans45.org/spurgeon/treasury/ps111.htm.
3. "promise". Dictionary.com. *Dictionary.com Unabridged*. Random House, Inc. http://dictionary.reference.com/browse/promise (accessed: December 22, 2015).
4. Bill Johnson, Twitter feed, @billjohnsonBJM, ca[2015].
5. Brian Houston, *Live, Love, Lead* (New York: Hachette Book Group, Inc., 2015).
6. Peter Toggs, Twitter feed, @PetertToggs ca[2015].
7. Samuel Chand (quoting Sheryl Brady), *Leadership Pain: The Classroom for Growth* (Nashville, Thomas Nelson Inc., 2015).

Chapter 4—Say YES to a Prosperous Soul

1. Watchman Nee, *The Salvation of the Soul*, (New York: Christian Fellowship Publishers, Inc., 1978). All rights reserved.

Chapter 5—Say YES to Being Shaken

1. Joey Bonifacio, *The Promise No One Wants*, http://joeybonifacio.com/bookbar/the-promise-no-one-wants/.

Chapter 6—Say YES to the Good Fight

1. John Wesley, *A Collection of Hymns for the Use of the People Called Methodists* (Originally published by Oxford University, 1804; digitized in 2006).
2. "siege", Strongs Concordance www.blueletterbible.org/lang/lexicon/lexicon
3. Bill Johnson – Twitter feed @billjohnsonBJM, ca[2015].
4. Eileen Crossman, *Mountain Rain* (Robesonia: OMF Books, 1987).
5. Author Unknown
6. Rick Johnston, quote from Servant Seminar, 1995.
7. "shield", International Standard Bible Dictionary, www.blueletterbible.org.
8. "helmet", International Standard Bible Dictionary, www.blueletterbible.org.
9. Francis Frangipane, *Three Battlegrounds* (Montgomery Village: Arrow Publications, Incorporated, 2006).
10. Graham Cook, Twitter feed, @GrahamCook, ca[2015].
11. E.M. Bounds, *Power Through Prayer* (New York: Cosimo Classics, ca{2007]

Chapter 7—Say YES to Your Place

1. Leonard Ravenhill, *Why Revival Tarries* (Bloomington: Bethany House Publishers, 1987).
2. Frank Damazio, *14 Tests All Leaders Must Face (Life Impact Series)* (Portland: City Bible Publishing, 2005).
3. Charles E Blair, TH.B., D.D., Litt.D., *New Spirit-Filled Life Bible* (Nashville: Thomas Nelson, Inc., 2002).
4. A. Coones Jr., Facebook post, https://www.facebook.com/arnie.coone ca[2015]. Used by Permission.
5. Frank Damazio, *From Barrenness to Fruitfulness* (Regal Books, 1998).
6. Ray Stedman, Ephesians – Commentary, www.blueletterbible.org.

Chapter 8—Say YES to the House of God

1. Brian Houston, Twitter feed, @BrianCHouston, ca[2015].

Chapter 9—Say YES to Reaching One Person at a Time

1. Penn Jillette, Penne Jillettes Podcast, Published on Nov 13, 2009, https://www.youtube.com/watch?v=owZc3Xq8obk
2. The Institute for American Church Growth, Copyright 1977-2005, Church Growth, Inc. All rights reserved.
3. Maya Angelou http://www.goodreads.com/quotes/5934-i-ve-learned-that-people-will-forget-what-you-said-people
4. Michael Camp, *The Leader in the Mirror* (Micheal Camp, 2010). All rights reserved.
5. Chris Hodges, Twitter feed, @Chris_Hodges, ca[2015

Made in the USA
San Bernardino, CA
25 July 2016